Your Dance Résumé

A Guide to Self-Marketing for Performers

Eric Wolfram

Dancepress Digital
New York, NY

This Book is dedicated to my
wonderful family and all the friends
who have helped me grow.

Published by Dancepress Digital
170 East 91st Street, #1W
New York, NY 10128 USA
c 1994, 2007

ISBN: 1-880404-06-0

Table of Contents

Your Dance Résumé

Acknowledgements

When it came time to write this book, I realized my network of help extended far beyond what I had any right to ask. Glen Edgeston, Wayne Eagling, Maina Gielgud, Roy Kaisel, Kevin Mckenzie, Arthur Mitchell, Lawrence Rhodes, Francia Russell, Ben Stevenson, Paul Taylor, Helgi Tomasson, Edward Villella, Karen P. Brown, Peter Diggins, and Mark Kappel—thank you for answering the director's poll and thanks to your staff for completing the other material. Merle Hubbard, thank you for revealing the three magic words. Thanks to Dance Magazine and Hanna Rubin for allowing me to reprint my article on Video marketing.

I was blessed with many friends and colleagues who selflessly offered to help with this project. Mikko Nissinen, Blanca Coma, Otis Thomson, Pete Iaria, Katita Waldo, Julia Barrick Taffe, Richard McLeod, Charles David Anderson, Anthony Randazzo, Jennifer Blake, Rodolphe Cassand, Rachel Greenwood, Jais Zinoun, David Palmer, Edward W. Pearlstien, Susan Kelley, Ben McDonald, Griff Lopez, Jose Martin, Askia Swift, Deirdre Chapman, Virginia Long, and Peter Brandenhoff—thank you for your assistance, résumés, and proofreading help. Thank you Neva Beach for the editorial help and Otis Thomson for the graphic design. Thanks to Lily Seo and Catlin Kirschenbaum for permission to use their photos as good examples of audition photos.

Introduction

Dancers don't like to read. They respond to images of beauty, not to words; and I'm not going to argue that point because the proof is in the bookstores. The dance section, if there is one, is a shelf half-filled with books full of pictures. The few exceptions are the books written by celebrities, which also appeal to the non-dancing public – people who like to read stories about the twisted lives of dancers on their graves, or the biographies of choreographic geniuses like Mark Morris.

Dancers don't write much either. In twelve years as a professional dancer, I was never asked to write anything. Furthermore, dancers start young. Their adolescent focus is on training and rehearsals, which end at 10:30 p.m.; not on grammar teachers who, bless their souls, tend to ramble on about predicates and indirect objects. Dancers ignore writing. This truism would be laughable if it were not so serious. So how is a dancer supposed to write a good résumé. We used the following method.

The day before an audition, we'd ask someone to borrow a résumé, and then we'd copy it. The result depended on the quality of the résumé we copied. Others would have their fathers, who never seem understand that heights and weights are important to an artistic director, write their résumés. The results tend to be corporate forms, highlighting college training (a big no-no) and not the most important roles that the dancers performed. I knew there had to be a better way.

So where does a dancer go when it comes time to audition? My answer is here, a book called Your Dance Résumé.

Chapter 1

Self-Marketing for Dancers

Whatever you can do,
or dream you can, begin it.
Boldness has genius, power, and
magic in it.
GOETHE

What is a dance résumé?

Your dance résumé is your own personal advertisement. It is the centerpiece of your audition package, which includes a cover letter, photos and perhaps a video, reviews if you have them, and references.

Your résumé is intended to sell your services to the artistic director of a dance company or to a choreographer. It's neither an autobiography nor a methodical listing of every role you have ever performed. It's a carefully selected and formulated document that distills and highlights your accomplishments and experience to serve your current dance goals.

In researching this web page, a questionnaire was sent to the artistic directors of some of the most respected dance companies of the world. Almost all of the directors agreed that the résumés they receive are poorly done—sloppy, amateurish, confusing, too full of details or too skimpy—and sometimes all at once. Their message is clear: you can set yourself apart from the competition by presenting yourself professionally on paper.

There isn't one correct way to write a résumé, only better ways. This guide is designed to help you write a résumé that is a true reflection of yourself and the services you wish to contribute to the world of dance.

Do Your Best

Whenever you do anything, you should try hard to do it right. This is particularly true when writing a résumé. A résumé should be perfect—it's as simple as that. Your first impression on the artistic director depends upon it.

Your résumé package makes a personal statement about you. If your résumé is casual, sloppy, and confused, it suggests that your dancing will be too. It implies that you aren't motivated to do your best, or that you don't care about the impression you make. It can cost you a job.

In contrast, a focused, clean, well-written résumé sends a completely different message to your potential employer. It shows that you respect yourself and the director, and are a professional. It can land you a job.

If you're going about this in a rush, slow down. Take the time you need to do the job properly. Like dancing, writing a résumé simply requires the commitment to do your best and the persistence to keep going until you've succeeded.

Reach for the stars and they can be yours. Imagine a successful audition, the beginning of a wonderful future. Dream of what you will become as you're molded into the finest of dancers. Then present yourself on paper in a way that not only reflects your excellence in dance but your spirit, desires, and professionalism.

Your résumé is no place for modesty, so get out of that frame of mind right now if you're in it. It's alright to be vain on your résumé, this is where you should shine as brightly as you can.

Fall down seven times, get up eight.
JAPANESE PROVERB

Chapter 2

Doing the Research

You've got to be very careful if

you don't know where you're

going, because you might not get there.
YOGI BERRA

Where are you going?

Before you begin writing your résumé, you must consider where it will be sent. A résumé is most effective if it is designed to fit a specific target—the company or school where you intend to seek an audition.

Researching your target company (or companies) is crucial. It lets you personalize the résumé and cover letter, which not only flatters the recipient, but demonstrates your profound interest in their organization.

Even the simplest details are important. Most people dislike having their name misspelled, for instance, and directors are no different. You must determine the name of the artistic director and his or her company, and the correct spelling of both. Beyond that, find out as much as you possibly can. The time you spend doing a complete investigation is always worth it.

In addition to the director's name and its spelling, find out where he or she danced, where he or she studied dance, how long he or she has been director, and what repertoire he or she has added during his or her tenure. Know the name of the assistant director, the length of the contract, the location of the company, where the company tours, and a complete list of the company's repertoire for at least the last four years.

Where to start?

The Internet is the best place to start. Cyberdance.org has a fairly comprehensive listing of the web sites of dance companies. Then go to Google and search the names of artistic directors and the teachers at the places you're interested in. Additional sources of information are articles published in Dance Magazine, reviews in the New York Times, and books about the company's history. Go to the library and look at the back issues of Dance Magazine to find any mention of your target company. You can also search Dance Magazine's Annual Directory here: dancemagazine.com/dance_annual/search/

Make sure you lurk on news groups like, alt.arts.ballet and rec.arts.dance. Read the excellent FAQ which includes a listing of the entire dance related web pages, frequently asked questions about dance, and a list of books available on the subject. If this seems like a daunting task, ask a computer-competent friend to print all the information you need.

Call each of your target companies and ask for the person in charge of public relations. The larger companies will have separate production offices, which will gladly assist you, but even the smallest companies will have someone who deals with public relations. Politely explain that you are a dancer interested in auditioning for their company, and that you would like information about their repertoire for the past five years and the repertoire the company intends to dance this season. Also ask for the director's biography, where the company is planning to tour, and to whom you should send your audition materials.

One of the best ways to discover information is to talk to someone in the company, or someone who has been in the company, preferably a dancer. The dance world is so small that if you don't know someone in your target company, you probably know someone who knows someone in that company. It's just a matter of a little research. Once you find someone 'in the loop', ask him or her some questions like:

What are the classes like?
Who teaches?
What is the director like?
How are the dancers treated and addressed?
How hard is the workload?
Do you know of anyone who is planning to leave after this season?
What is the range of salaries?
What time of year do the dancers return their letters of intent?

The letter of intent is a letter from the artistic director indicating his intent to re-engage a dancer for the next season. It must be signed and returned to the director, which indicates the dancer's wish to stay another season. The directors know how many contracts must be filled after the dancers return their letters of intent. Obviously, the best time to have your résumé land on an artistic director's desk is soon after the letters of intent are returned, because that's when he or she discovers that a new dancer is needed.

Doing this research is valuable for more than writing a good résumé. If you like what you discover about the company, the new knowledge will cement your determination, intensify your desire for success, and therefore compel you to follow through and do your best. On the other hand, such a complete investigation might uncover reasons to drop the company from your audition list and save time, money, and effort.

Little bits of information are nuggets of gold when used to personalize a résumé and cover letter. Mentioning specific details of a company is not only flattering and interesting to a director; it shows him or her your keen interest in the company and the intensity of your desire to audition for it.

I once discovered that an artistic director had spent many years in Munich. I mentioned my recent audition at Bayerisches Staatsballet in the cover letter and when I called, that's all he could talk about. He couldn't wait to see me in an audition, and when we met, he treated me like an old friend.

Chapter 3

Résumé Basics

Success is not the result
of spontaneous combustion.
You must set yourself on fire.
REGGIE LEACH

The résumé is the centerpiece of a dancer's audition package. Yet if you could look through the résumés sent to any large American ballet company, you'd see that most of them are not very good. They lack neatness, focus, impact, and precision. Important information is often absent or hard to find, while unnecessary details clutter the page. Many dance companies are overwhelmed with hundreds of such résumés each season. Keep this in mind when you write your own. Even in such a large crowd you can stand out if your résumé is better than the rest—just as you'd hope to stand out on stage by dancing with more dynamics, precision, and control then the other dancers.

What should you include in a résumé and what should you leave out? Read on.

A Dance Résumé Always Includes:

1. Name, address, and phone number
Although the reasons for including this information are obvious, it is surprising how many people forget to incorporate it in their résumés.

The people who leave this information off their résumé don't get very far in their search for a job. Many dancers use a stage name; use it on your résumé if you have one.

2. **Date of birth**
Although your birth date is not usually required on résumés for traditional jobs, most artistic directors want to know your age. This is usually because they have some policy, written or unwritten, about how old a dancer at a particular level should be. If you think your age might be a problem, call to learn the guidelines. Fear of age discrimination has compelled many dancers to lie about their age on a résumé. Don't do this unless you are prepared to live a lie in pursuit of your dreams. Management does not appreciate dishonesty and the disrespect, which accompanies deceit. It is true that people have traditionally lied about their age on their dance résumés in the past and have gotten away with it, partly because once a dancer is beyond the audition process and into the school or company, the staff has had the time to grow to admire the dancer's talent or potential. At this point they are more likely to forgive other, less fortunate aspects of the dancer's overall circumstances. You probably won't be fired for lying on a résumé. Understand that if you lie, however, your secret will eventually be discovered and people will talk about your true age—behind your back and in your face.

3. **Weight and height**
Your weight and height are also important. Leaving these statistics off your résumé looks suspicious. There is no need for fractions in height or weight. If you are 5'8 3/4" tall and want to appear shorter on your résumé, write 5'8". On the other hand, if you're 5'11 1/2" and think you are more marketable at an even 6', then round up.

4. **Citizenship**
Indicate your citizenship with your height and weight. This information is important to directors, who must deal with visas and quotas. If you are auditioning in America as a foreigner, but have a green card or a visa to work in America, then absolutely include that information in addition to, or instead, of your nationality.

5. Company names
Unless you have been in a lot of different companies in the last two years or are writing a purely functional résumé, include the names of all the companies for which you have worked.

6. Featured roles
Include the names of ballets, the choreographers, and roles you have danced. However, if you have ample professional experience it's counterproductive to list every role you have ever danced, because your featured roles will be lost in the clutter of your smaller roles. If this is your case, it's more effective to only list your "Featured Roles". If you have very little stage time or no professional experience, include all your dance experience on your résumé.

7. Education
This refers to where you learned to dance, not your high school. Start with the most recent school you attended and work backwards.

The more professional experience a dancer has, the less important his or her training becomes. A dancer straight out of school with no professional experience should put an education section right after their career highlights section. You may include information about a school you attended, even if you did not graduate from its program. If you received a scholarship, it shows that the organization had confidence in your ability to succeed as a dancer, so be sure to highlight such honors boldly on your résumé.

What about small workshops, like that two-week workshop on East Indian dancing you took five years ago? Ask yourself, "How does this schooling apply to my current career goals?" If you are auditioning for a show called Shiva-The Indian God of Dance, information about this workshop could be placed confidently at the top your résumé. However, this information has no place on a résumé for a Broadway show, because someone casting A Chorus Line might have little interest in the state of your mantras.

8. Other awards
You should include any awards, certification honors, and medals you received from competitions or examinations. The results of a Cecchetti

exam become less important as a dancer becomes more established and should fade to the bottom of their résumé as their experience section fills out. On the other hand, a first place award on Star Search might be the distinction that separates your résumé from the pile.

We forfeit three-fourths of
ourselves to be like other people
ARTHUR SCHOPENHAUER

A Résumé Sometimes Includes:

1. Choreographic creations
Definitely include this if research of the target company revealed that the resident choreographer requires improvisation technique from their dancers. Many modern companies encourage their dancers to choreograph, or at least see it as a positive sign, so for them you might include this information, especially if it doesn't push your résumé into a second or third page. On the other hand, many ballet companies and casting agents don't really care about their dancers' choreographic dreams, and would actually dislike it if a dancer became too creative with the given steps.

2. Acting experience
Again, if it doesn't push you to the next page, then go ahead and include it, especially if you have some impressive screen or stage experience. If you are auditioning for a musical or an opera and think some acting might be required, then of course you should include this sort of work.

3. Musical Training
Most dancers have had some musical training. Furthermore, many prospective employers are disinterested in the three years of piano classes you took when you were a pre-teen. Unless your training is extensive and you have won some award or distinguished yourself in the field of music, or unless you need to beef up your résumé because

you have virtually no dance experience, it is better to leave your musical training off the résumé.

4. References
A better place to indicate a reference is in the cover letter or on a separate sheet of paper in the résumé package, but you may include this information on your résumé, especially if you have a reference who is known and trusted by the target director. Be sure to let the reference know they might be contacted and take a moment to fill them in on your activities since you last saw them.

> *Drawing on my fine command*
> *of the English language,*
> *I said nothing.*
> **ROBERT BENCHLEY**

A Résumé Should Not Include:

1. Anything negative
Everyone has limitations, but a résumé is not the place to confess them. Any shortcomings that you have can be toned down by your résumé. However, do not highlight your weaknesses by mentioning them on your résumé. Often, for a director, résumé reading is a process of elimination; don't give him or her a reason not to call you back. Never mention bad experiences with former directors, choreographers, or teachers. It might indicate that *you* have the bad attitude.

2. Hair and eye color
None of the directors I surveyed thought this information served them at all. For this reason, it's not necessary to give your hair and eye color.

3. The word résumé
Your résumé should look like a résumé, and if it doesn't, then it should be rewritten. A title at the top saying "R E S U M E" or "Professional Profile" is simply redundant.

4. **Reasons for leaving a job**

If prospective employers want to know why you left or are leaving a job, then they can ask you. If they do ask why you are leaving your job, be sure not to give any negative reason. It's much better to say, "I need a change so that I may continue to grow, "rather than, "I feel suffocated at my current company because the director treats me unfairly." Negative comments reflect poorly on you. In any case, a résumé is not the place to defend your reasons for leaving a job.

5. **Salary requirements**

Although it is sometimes helpful for a director to know what position a dancer is auditioning for, the résumé is not intended to begin negotiations for a salary. Once a director has offered you a contract, then you might consider negotiating a more substantial salary. In that case talk with the general manager, not the director. Listing your compensation expectations on your résumé will only serve to limit your chances for an audition, by either lowering the quality of your résumé with this inappropriate demand, or by simply pricing yourself out of the job.

Chapter 4

Advanced Résumé

> *I always wanted to be*
> *somebody but I should*
> *have been more specific.*
> **HELEN KELLER**

The most effective résumés focus on the employer and what he or she needs, rather than on your past. A wise dancer looks carefully at the repertoire he or she has danced, the companies performed with, and the schools he or she has attended to find common connections with the target director.

Some artistic directors would be thrilled to know that the person auditioning has seen their choreographic works before, and are therefore aware of the type of dancing they would be doing. In addition, mentioning teachers or choreographers known to the artistic director provides interest and points of reference to the director, and for this reason should be highlighted in the résumé or cover letter. Such information can be given either in the résumé or the cover letter; to help you chose where, refer to the case studies and samples> to see various ways and places to include it.

The Main Question

Imagine you have already sent your résumé to your target company, and by coincidence the director is answering his or her own mail on the day it arrives. Here is the chance you've been waiting for—an actual, living, breathing director is looking at your résumé, someone who might even call you for an audition. What should your résumé be saying? If a director is looking at your résumé, he or she will be searching for one answer: What can you do for my company?

What can you do for my company? At first glance, that question might sound obvious. Upon re-examination, notice how standard résumés only answer this question in an indirect manner. Think about it: Most résumés are a chronological summary of what you have done. The director must look at your experience, evaluate the significance of your achievements, and, finally, put it all onto a scale to understand where you belong in his or her own company. Instead of making a long, self-absorbed testament of your dance career, it behooves you to answer the director's question.

Your résumé can do this in two ways: first, by stating what service you are offering boldly at the top of your résumé and, second, by presenting it in a way that lets him or her see you in the best possible light. If you want to dance in the target company—say it. If you want a corps de ballet job—say it. If you are willing to apprentice—say it, and by all means, if you are only going to accept a certain level, don't be afraid to say it. This is one way to format your résumé to serve the person who is hiring.

Now it's your turn!

On a separate piece of paper list:

* Every role you have ever danced.

* Every company you have worked for and the dates you worked there.

* The dance schools, programs, and workshops you attended and the dates you were there.

* Any awards or scholarships you have received.

* Any roles that were created for you.

* All film or stage acting experience.

* List anyone you have worked with who also knows your target director.

* Look at the repertoire of your target company and list any works from it you have done.

* List choreography you've danced that is traditionally danced by the school or company attended by the target director. For instance, a director who has worked with Jose Limon will be interested if you have danced The Moor's Pavan, and a director who has studied at the School of the Royal Danish Ballet has a clear frame of reference and understanding of the Bournonville style.

What are your most important accomplishments with each company or school you attended, such as:

Lead roles, first cast performances, quick promotions, renown partners, outstanding exams, working with special choreographers, and recognitions or awards.

It is a good idea to obey all
the rules when you're young
just so you'll have the strength
to break them when you're old.

MARK TWAIN

The Format

If you ask one hundred people how to organize and present the information in a résumé, you will get one hundred different answers. One person will tell you the exact opposite of another. So much depends on how this résumé helps achieve your goal. This is the most important message on this web page. You'll want a different résumé for different occasions. One résumé might be fan-fair or hype, intended for the press, sales material, or your biography on the inside of a program. Another résumé, intended to land a teaching job at a university, might be in c.v. format, listing your college education first, followed by every dance related event in which you've participated. Seeking a gig in a TV commercial, you might list your film experience first, and for a ballet gig, you might leave this information off entirely.

Nevertheless, there are two common and accepted approaches to writing a résumé: the chronological method and the functional method. The format you decide to use should reflect your personality and be tailored to fit the specific organization to which your résumé is being sent. Use the method that you are most comfortable with, and, more importantly the method which best showcases your background and experience. Someone who has little professional experience might try a functional résumé, which highlights skills rather than work history.

Look at the sample résumés and read the following descriptions to understand the advantages and disadvantages of each method.

The Chronological Method

The chronological method is the most conservative and widely accepted format for a résumé. Its distinguishing feature is that it lists your most recent work experience at the top, and continues down in chronological order. Its main advantage is that it highlights a strong, steady work history while providing the director complete information about your past. It also is a method many people are familiar with, and it's easy to prepare in a logical manner. If your most relevant dance experience was long ago, don't be afraid to put it at the top of the résumé and list your additional work experience in chronological order to end with your current job.

This method tends to highlight the dates of employment and the companies you have worked for rather then the specific roles you have danced or the specific choreographers with whom you have worked.

Actually, where you have danced is far more important then when you danced there. The dates aren't nearly as important as what you have danced and what you are capable of dancing. For this reason your résumé is better if it has the dates on the far right margin like examples. Or you can simply omit the dates entirely by using the functional method.

The Functional Method

Unfortunately, a person with no work history, a disastrous employment background, or who started dancing seriously late will only highlight these weaknesses with the chronological method. These potential barriers to employment can be minimized with the functional method. Furthermore, older dancers who wish to conceal their age, but feel uncomfortable changing dates around to accommodate an artificial age, find the functional format most congenial.

The primary distinction of the functional method is that the work history section is completely omitted. You list only the talents and experiences most relevant to the position you are seeking, regardless of your work history. Although this method works well for people who have just graduated from school and have no professional experience, it can be used effectively by anyone, especially those who have gaps in their dance history, or have a confusing or limited employment background.

One of the advantages of this method is it gives you complete control over how you present yourself. It allows you to creatively display your most notable experience in a unique manner. The primary disadvantage of the functional method is it might create suspicion in the employer's mind about the lack of complete information.

A combination of the chronological method and the functional method is also possible. Basically, such a résumé highlights where and when you have worked, without submitting to the rigid chronological format, while still granting you some of the freedoms offered by the functional format. This method is a favorite with many dancers.

If you are using a functional format, it is often effective to write your résumé in the third person, as in "Ms. Goldstein performed Charity in the world première of Sweet Charity II," or even the first person, as in "I studied dance at the University of California." For a conservative or chronological résumé, it is congruent with the style to write in a voice which implies the subject, such as "Successfully premièred as Janis in the critically acclaimed Dance of Time," or "Featured in Swan Lake as the Jester."

Chapter 5

Your Writing Style

The future belongs to those who
Believe in the beauty of their dreams.
ELEANOR ROOSEVELT

The method you use is a matter of style—your style. Look at the samples and ask yourself which résumé style suits you best.

Make sure your writing is direct and simple. It is difficult to explain what constitutes a good writing style. You might sense your writing isn't good but can't seem to fix it, just as someone who isn't a dancer knows "this dancer is better then that one" but often can't explain why. If you're motivated to improve your writing, Strunk and White's The Elements of Style and William Zinsser's On Writing Well, are good places to start. Otherwise, have your résumé read by someone who knows about writing.

If you are at all unsure about your writing, consider hiring a professional to re-write your cover letter and résumé. Look for editorial services in the yellow pages, on bulletin boards at universities, or in weekly community papers. You can also try looking on craigslist.org. Tell them you want your résumé and cover letter rewritten and edited. You can have this done for between ten and forty dollars. Don't confuse editing services with résumé-writing services which interview you to create your package for you. Such services might ask as much as $250-$500 to write your résumé. There are a lot of bad editors who are only trying to make a quick buck and couldn't care less about the finished product, so watch out. Ask for references and check up on them. A good editor will have many satisfied customers.

You can also ask a friend to help you with your writing. Sometimes it is better to have someone else write about you. He or she will bring a new perspective to your résumé. But make sure you like what the person is writing because it is your résumé after all.

Use of one of the three magic words described in the next section to make your résumé and cover letter even more powerful. After discovering which magic word fits you best, look at the list of words which can add personality and spice to your résumé package.

Ah, but a man's reach should exceed

his grasp, or what is a heaven for?

ROBERT BROWNING

Chapter 6

The Three Magic Words
(And Their Hundred and Fifty-Five Little Helpers)

Nothing contributes so much to
tranquilize the mind as a steady purpose—
a point on which the soul may fix it's intellectual eye
MARY WOLLSTONECRAFT SHELLEY

The three magic words are:

1. Promises.
2. Emerging.
3. Demonstrated.

You start with promise. If you have absolutely no professional experience, you still have promise. This can be written in your résumé with passages like:

Because of his natural partnering abilities, his dedicated work habit, slender legs, and voluptuous arches, Mr. Lee promises to be a recognized classical dancer.

Once you are established as a dancer, you graduate to "emerging." You can also use some of its synonyms—rising, appearing, or dawning. Try this magic word in sentences like:

Emerging as an elegant and refined technician whose immaculate style woos the audience into ovations.

The final step, reserved for seasoned professionals, is "demonstrated." Demonstrated and its synonyms—shown, confirmed, or proven—are powerful words. Write "have demonstrated" on your résumé and you almost don't need to write anything else. Try it in paragraphs like:

Victoria has demonstrated her artistry in theaters throughout the world. She has proven herself to be a leading artist and a box office draw.

While it's definitely nice to say you "have demonstrated" on your résumé, it's certainly dignified to "be emerging" or to "be promising." This is the one place on your résumé where you can be a bit modest and still not sell yourself short.

One dancer asked, "I've been emerging for my whole career. When will I graduate to 'have demonstrated?'" When you're good enough—that's when.

A Hundred and Fifty-Five Little Helpers

Here is a list of words that will add color, power and impact to your résumé and cover letter. Use them sparingly, perhaps one or two, and make sure you look them up in a dictionary before you do. Sometimes the definition will be different then you had imagined.

A Guide to Self-Marketing for Performers

Magic	Vibrant	Exuberant	Exhilarated	Phenomenal
Perfect	Focused	Explosive	Brilliant	Gifted
Ecstatic	Confident	Determined	Fast	Serene
Impassioned	Ballistic	Motivated	Driven	Compelled
Centered	Achieved	Created	Recognized	Supported
Participated	Performed	Produced	Promoted	Irresistible
Enchanting	Gracious	Bewitching	Captivating	Versatile
Original	Spectacular	Abundant	Successfully	Respected
Accomplished	Illustrious	Notable	Esteemed	Dominant
Prestigious	Influential	Absorbing	Gripping	Overwhelming
Provocative	Fascinating	Seductive	Talented	Seasoned
Ace	Master	Capable	Veteran	Proficient
Alluring	Dynamic	Dramatic	Intoxicating	Incisive
Enlivened by	Qualified	Flair for	Solid experience	Endowed with
The artistry of	Competence	Finesse	Magnificent	Dazzling
Splendid	Unforgettable	Sensational	Majestic	Glorious
Light	Soft	Dainty	Clean	Natural
Immaculate	Refreshing	Exhilarating	Pristine	Playful
Integrity	Revealing	Unequivocal	Reputable	Perfected
Transformed	Enriched	Indispensable	Imperative	Essential
Significant	Invaluable	Vital	Enlightening	Illuminating
Precious	Superb	Elegant	Classic	Rare
Elite	Posh	Refined	Innovative	Revolutionary
Modern	Ultramodern	Sophisticated	Futuristic	Favorite
Famous	Famed	Legendary	Celebrated	Illustrious
Riveting	Vitality	Vigor	Potent	Intense
Rugged	Dependable	Practical	Strong	Trusted
Established	Pursue	Peerless	Gorgeous	Appealing
Alluring	Vivid	Sheer	Prestige	Petite
Slim	First rate	Chic	Supreme	Slender
Outrageous	Bold	Daring	Graceful	First class

Your Dance Résumé

Chapter 7

The Elements of a Résumé

*Don't play for safety—it's the
most dangerous thing
in the world.*
Hugh Walpole

Headings

It is helpful to organize your career information into groups, each
under a heading such as: Objective, Career Highlights or Summary of
Qualifications, Professional Experience or Experience, and Dance
Education or Training. This will make your résumé more readable and
allow you to show off your most important accomplishments in a
fashion both professional and tasteful.

Objective Heading

Some résumés include a section labeled "Objective" or "Career Goal".
One of the most common debates about résumés is whether or not to
include an objective section. Some people use this heading and others
do not. It's a matter of style. Here is a chance to clearly indicate your
intentions.

Career Highlights Heading

The next heading is the Career Highlights or Summary of Qualifications section. This is an opportunity to boldly state the best of your career, your most shining moments, right at the top of your résumé, regardless of whether they happened yesterday or seven years ago. When this section is omitted and a strictly chronological format is used, important information can get buried under years of other, less impressive, experience. Avoid simply listing your featured roles in a boring fashion.

Boring:

Appeared in Mark Martin's Hail Storm.

Better:

Was selected by Mark Martin to be first cast in the premier performance of his critically acclaimed Hail Storm for the Los Angeles Ballet.

Boring:

Worked for Linda Simmer in her Choreographic Experience.

Better:

Worked with Linda Simmer to create a solo and duet for her Eight Plus One, in addition to being responsible to understudy three other roles in the same ballet.

It is up to you to see your experience objectively and describe it in a compelling fashion. Do not lie, but don't sell yourself short either. In a résumé it is sometimes difficult to tell where humility stops and egotism begins, but being modest can leave you on the outside looking in. There is a fine line between selling yourself and boasting. Choreographers and directors don't want trouble from pushy prima

donnas so outright bragging is not good policy. However, make an
effort to see your accomplishments objectively, then write a résumé
which states your experience and level confidently and with dignity.

Professional Experience Heading

The next section on your résumé is the experience section where you
list the companies you've worked for and some of the roles you've
danced. You can enliven this area as well.

Boring:

The Great Gatsby	Daisy	J. Hoover	
Cinderella	Cinderella	R. Robins	
Taming of the Shrew	Pas de six	J. Hanko	
Nutcracker	Snow Queen	B. Houston	
Flower Soldier Parent			
Symphony in B	Demi-soloist	G. Blanch	Corps

Better:

Featured as a soloist by Imre Dovella in a variety of principal roles,
which include: Daisy in A. Hoover's The Great Gatsby, Cinderella in
R. Robin's production of Cinderella, Snow Queen in Ben Houston's
Nutcracker, first movement demi-soloist in George Blanch's
Symphony in B, and many other roles choreographed by Mr. Dovella.

If, for some reason (perhaps a grant application), you must list every
role you ever danced, and insist on doing so in a cold, methodical
manner, the title of the work is in italics, the name of the
choreographer follows in parenthesis (first name or initial can be given
to add clarity), and the role is next, such as:

Boring:

Fez Ballet 1986-1989

Swan Lake (Petipa) Odette

Fathom of a Heart (Wolf) Blue couple

Holding On (Holdin) Soloist

Ya Ka Bimmbo (Washington) Pas de deux

Fall River Legend (De Mille) Lizzy

Freemont Ballet 1989-1996

What To Do Till The

Train Comes Back

to Houston (Lopez) Messiah

Who Killed Bobby More? (Zimmerman) The Agent

Note: Your web browser might change the format, so read the above paragraph carefully.

Dance Training Heading

A section for education follows the experience section. Here it is also more impressive if you do more than just list your schools or teachers.

Boring:

Alabama School of Fine Arts

Lorna Fordyce Dance Studio

Better:

Attended and graduated from Alabama School of Fine Arts. Passed all the required dance and musical training exams. Received intensive technique training from Lorna Fordyce in San Francisco.

Boring:

Grinko Winnie, Carl Mononi, Sandy Eppenheimer, Otis Thomson, and Uggie Johnson.

Better:

Trained in classical ballet by former NYBT II ballet mistress Grinko Winnie and renowned Italian teacher Carl Mononi. Introduced to modern technique by Sandy Eppenheimer and Otis Thomson, and studied composition from choreographer Uggie Johnson.

Now it's your turn!

Objective

Decide if you are going to use an objective or career goal heading on your résumé. Phrase your objective specifically as possible. Study the sample résumés ideas.

Career Highlights or Summary of Qualifications

Pick one of the following headings to highlight up to three of your most important experiences:

1. Career Highlights
2. Summary of Qualifications
3. Featured Roles
4. Outstanding Achievements
5. Experience

6.   Summary of Experience

Write a compelling and honest paragraph for each of your highlights.

Experience and Education

Study the sample résumés in the back of this book. On a separate piece of paper, write your experience and education section. Use one or two words from the magic list.

Remember a résumé is intended to summarize a dancer's education and experience, and to be submitted in application for a job. What you leave off your résumé is just as important as what you include. Your dance résumé should quickly provide the information necessary for the director to understand how you might potentially fit on his or her stage. It should logically build upon and support itself to create the impression of intelligence, and imply that you know this profession very well and are committed to dancing your best.

Destiny is not a matter of chance,
it is a matter of choice; it is not a
thing to be waited for, it is a
thing to be achieved.

WILLIAM JENNINGS BRYAN

Chapter 8

The Cover Letter

Saddle your dreams afore you ride 'em.
MARY WEBB
1881-1927

The cover letter is as important as the résumé itself, and is perhaps the most consequential letter a dancer writes (for many dancers it's the only letter they ever write.) Often your first contact with the director, a well-written cover letter makes the most of that all-important first impression. It can significantly improve your chances for an audition by generating excitement and interest. If poorly written, it can be devastating to an otherwise well-formulated self-marketing campaign.

Few dancers invest enough time and care in preparing the cover letter. Many even omit it entirely. This is a serious mistake. A résumé arriving on the directors' desk without a cover letter that explains why it is being sent leaves the director wondering what the exact intent of the dancer is; it is not always obvious. Does she want to audition for the school? Does she want to audition for the company? Is she coming tomorrow? Does she want me to call her? Should I throw this résumé away? These are some questions that might pop-up if you don't include a cover letter.

So never underestimate the power of the cover letter. Since your future job may be riding on it, take the time and care necessary to write this crucial element of your résumé package. Make the most of this chance to stir interest in you as a possible new member of the company.

Basically, a cover letter does three things:

* Serves as a transmittal letter for your résumé.

* Introduces you and your outstanding dance achievements to the director.

* Generates interest in you and compels the director to take an action that will put you closer to an audition.

Understand, your cover letter not only introduces you, your résumé, and your experience to the director, but also acts as a sales letter which convinces the director you have something valuable to offer the company. The appearance of the cover letter should be as flawless as the résumé, because it also makes a statement about you to your prospective employer. If it is sloppy, rushed, and unfocused, it will imply that your dancing is sloppy and unfocused. It may also suggest that you are lazy and have little self-respect. It's as if you showed up at an audition wearing torn tights and a smelly, ragged leotard. Have some self-respect! A well-written cover letter will also suggest that you are professional, diligent, and confident.

The Form of a Business Letter

The cover letter is best written in the form of a business letter. This creates a neat, positive image, enhances readability, and shows that you care about the look of your résumé package. After reading what is included in a business letter read the dancer's step-by-step tricks to writing an effective cover letter.

A business letter contains the following elements in the order of their appearance on the letter:

1. **Return address-** The return address is single-spaced and, depending on the length of the letter, about five to ten lines from the top of the page. It is flush with the right margin.

2. **Date-** The date of the letter is positioned on the next line below the return address. The month is capitalized and never abbreviated.

3. **Address-** This includes the name of the person to whom the letter is sent, his or her title, the name of the company, and the organization's full mailing address.

4. **Salutation-** This is a greeting to the person whom you are writing. For example:

> Dear Mr. Martin:
>
> Dear Ms. Stealer:
>
> Dear John,

Don't use the director's first name unless you have been introduced in person and are on a first-name basis. Even then, weigh the closeness of your relationship before following this practice. Use a colon if you have never met the person and use a comma if you have.

Try to avoid such salutations as:

> Dear Sir or Madam:
>
> To whom it may concern:
>
> Dear director:

There is no reason to use such impersonal greetings. It is important to show interest in the company, and with a minimum effort you can find the name of the director.

5. **Body-** The body of the letter starts two spaces beneath the salutation, and contains your message to the director. The text is single-spaced, with a double space between paragraphs. (More on this important part of the cover letter later.)

6. **Closing-** Sincerely, Sincerely yours, and Most sincerely are appropriate closings for use with persons who are unknown to you. Best wishes, Yours, and Best regards are somewhat informal and normally reserved for persons with whom you have a fairly close relationship. The closing is always followed by a comma and the first letter is always capitalized.

7. **The signature line-** The signature line is always flush with the closing and at four to six lines below it. It is your full name, with middle initial if applicable. Sign your full name unless you are on familiar terms with the addressee. In this case, just signing your first name or nickname often softens the formal nature of a business letter.

The Elements of an Effective Cover Letter

Following the five basic elements of an effective letter. Have a strong introductory paragraph that generates interest and either states or implies that your are seeking employment. Then a paragraph which highlights your key strengths and outstanding features, and a paragraph summarizing your education and performing experience. Most importantly, follow your history with a paragraph that compels the director to take an action that will lead to an eventual audition. Finally, include a statement of appreciation for the director's time spent reviewing your résumé package.

Introduction:

The introduction must not only establish your interest in employment, but grab the reader's attention and compel him or her to read further. Here is where your research pays off. Anything you can do to make the letter more personalized and less like a form letter will make the letter more interesting for the director to read. In the introduction, it's also wise to indicate your intentions (reason for writing); this will help the director by making it easy to understand how you might help him or her. Do not be afraid to clearly indicate the position you want to audition for, especially if you omitted the objective section on your résumé. Not only is it less cryptic, it indicates firm goals, confidence, and an awareness of your level.

Use personal contacts to open the letter, with paragraphs, such as:

During a recent discussion with Truman Jones, I became aware of your desire to engage a tall, male principal dancer to partner my former colleague Susan Slipper. I am interested in talking with you about that position.

Use specific information about the company to create introductory paragraphs, like:

I read the article on your company in the December issue of Dance Magazine about your interest in developing young talent and bringing European works to Ballet Washington. As an enthusiastic young dancer who also loves the works of Cranks and Chilean, I found this article unusually interesting and it prompts me to ask for an audition with your company.

Don't underestimate the value of a well-written compliment, such as:

I have been watching Tanz Munchen transform into a world-class company under your direction, and I admire its position as the leading dance company in Germany. I would like to be a part of this exciting company and feel that I can further strengthen your ensemble. Enclosed, therefore, please find my photos and résumé.

It should be clear by now how an imaginative use of research in the opening paragraph of the cover letter will create interest, give a good first impression, and serve you rather nicely in your quest for employment.

Now it's your turn!

Use information you gathered about your target companies to create a compelling opening paragraph for your cover letter. Mention either a mutual acquaintance or specific information about the company, or start with a compliment. The opening paragraph must contain the reasons for which you are writing and the exact position in which you are interested.

Value and summary:

The next two paragraphs do two things. One paragraph describes professional experience which might be of value to the target director, and motivates him or her to invite you for an audition. The second paragraph is dedicated to giving a brief summary of dance education and experience, and might include the number of years you have danced or the teachers with whom you have studied. These two paragraphs provide your main opportunity to market yourself and address the reasons you would be useful to the director. Don't be afraid to highlight or repeat information that is already included on your résumé. Stress your qualifications and enthusiasm in a personal manner.

Now it's your turn!

Use the list of your experience and training, and your knowledge of the target company and its director, to write a compelling paragraph about your extraordinary talents and a short paragraph which summarizes your dance history. Study the examples of cover letters and model your letter after them.

Action paragraph:

So you've said you want to audition. You've mentioned your qualifications. Now what? The next paragraph is very important, because it compels the reader to take some kind of action that will help you get an audition. Here are some examples of action statements:

Please have your assistant call me if you are interested in seeing my performance video.

I would appreciate the opportunity to audition for your company during my planned trip to Atlanta, and will call you next week to determine your interest and, if appropriate, to arrange for the meeting.

Should you have an opening in your company, I would welcome the opportunity to work with you in class, so you may determine if I am appropriate for your choreography. I can be reached at (415) 945-9584, and look forward to hearing from you.

Even if it's simply to tell the secretary to expect your call, this significant paragraph forces the director to take an action, . More importantly, it indicates further communication which might save your résumé from the dreaded "permanent file" where it will have little chance of being seen by the director again.

Now it's your turn!

Write a commanding action paragraph. It must indicate further communications to come and ideally will prod the director to really consider having you audition.

Appreciation paragraph:

Most directors and choreographers are extremely busy, and it is a matter of courtesy to express your appreciation for the time they are taking to review your audition material. See the sample cover letters for some closing paragraph examples. Try to avoid the words "thank you in advance for...." Thank the director for reading the cover letter or for considering you for an audition, or simply thank him or her.

Now it's your turn!

Select a paragraph from the examples below.

1. Thank you for your consideration.

2. I appreciate your time and consideration.

3. Thank you.

4. Thank you for your consideration, and I look forward to hearing from you.

A good cover letter incorporates all of the above elements. The letter is always typed and has an attractive overall appearance. It uses proper grammar and punctuation, and has perfect spelling. The text is concise and does not ramble on. There is no bragging or use of gross exaggerations, nor is the tone too humble or falsely modest. Instead, a job- winning cover letter sounds confident and professional without seeming to be aggressive and pushy.

Make sure you proofread the letter as you do your résumé. Check once for content, once for grammar, and once for typing mistakes and misspelled words. Have someone else read it. Read it backwards often helps find mistakes that were missed.

There is no security on this
earth, there is only opportunity.

GENERAL DOUGLAS MACARTHUR

Your Dance Résumé

Chapter 9

Photos

Put all your eggs in one basket and
WATCH THAT BASKET!
MARK TWAIN

Part of a dancer's résumé package is the required photos. Dancers are judged not only by their movement quality, but by their body type and line. Employers who hire based mainly on an employee's appearance skate onto leagal thin-ice, but even F. Lee Bailey wouldn't try and build this case against the director of a dance company.

A picture tells a thousand words. You need photos which speak of a vibrant, gifted dancer. At the very least they should display a dancer with a clean line, a sense of aesthetics, and a trim, fit body.

Make sure the photos are current. If they are too old they will not show the improvements you have made in the time since they were taken. If you are out of shape and are using old photos to deceive the director, you will only create disappointment come audition day. No one will be hired on photos alone—everyone must be seen by the director.

The Body Shot

The most important photo in a résumé package is an 8x10 full-body shot, in a flattering dance position. You must look your best from head to toe. Although it is impossible to lie to the camera, you can and must help it to create the best image of you. What is your best position? Probably your favorite position. However, you might ask a trusted teacher for their opinion.

Do not send a photo which in some way reveals a weakness or imperfect line. If you like how high your leg is in a photo, but wish you had straightened your other leg, then don't send it—try again. It doesn't help you if your legs look great but your hands look like lobster claws or your feet look like giant cashew nuts. Choose the shot with a lower leg and relaxed facial expression instead of the one with an amazing extension and an upper body in the throws of a seizure.

If you have two body photos in different positions which are equally good, then go ahead and send both, but sending more than two body shots is usually unnecessary. One exception is a seasoned professional putting together a self-marketing brochure. A colleague of mine does just that quite effectively. The cover page is his head shot which is followed by his résumé, a body shot, a page of reviews, another body shot, more reviews, an action stage shot, a list of featured roles, and finally an impressive photo of him as Apollo (Balanchine). He uses this to secure guesting contracts and he says it works quite well. However, in most cases, one or two body shots are sufficient.

A Guide to Self-Marketing for Performers

Lily Seo   *Photo by: Rosalie O'Connor*

The Head Shot

The head shot is an effective self-marketing tool because it begins to associate your name with your face. Consequently, many dancers send an 8x10 head shot with their résumé. This photo is a helpful but not a mandatory element of your audition package. After a month of auditioning, a director might forget your name but remember your face. If the face isn't clear on the body shot, then absolutely consider a separate head shot. Let down your hair and wear make-up if you choose. It's not necessary to wear dance clothes for a head shot. A good photographer will have skills and techniques for making your head shot look better than you imagined.

The Photo Shoot

A photo shoot is like a performance; you should be warm, focused, centered, and determined to do your best. Try to have a shoot right after class, and avoid cold and damp locations.

Besides the photographer and you, a third person is necessary at the shoot. The third person's job is to scrutinize your positions for flaws, adjust your stance, and suggest new poses. The third person should be someone with extensive dance training and a good eye for detail. It also helps if he or she has an encouraging and positive attitude. You will be disappointed in the results of your photo shoot if you rely on a photographer, who has limited dance knowledge, to pose you. Let the photographer concentrate on the logistics of the shoot. Trust the photographer with his or her technical knowledge of cameras, not for an aesthetic opinion of dance poses. Your photo must convey a professional-level dancer, and this requires the trained eye of someone who is seasoned and mature in dance.

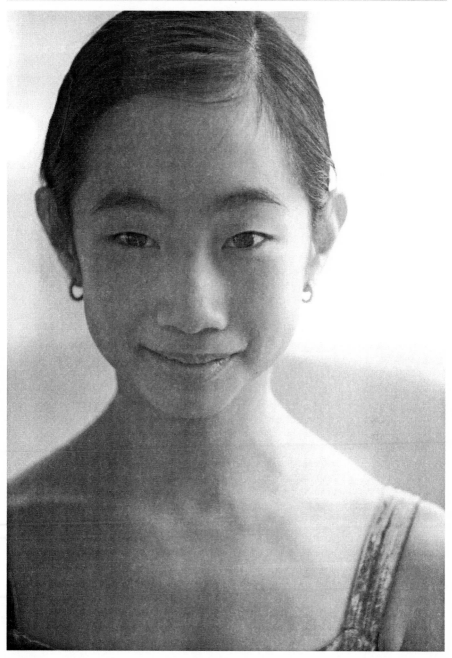

Lily Seo   *Photo by: Rosalie O'Connor*

Wear something that is tight-fitting and exhibits your body nicely. This can either be a costume, which looks very professional, or some clean, unripped rehearsal clothes in which you feel comfortable. Do not forget that the purpose of the body shot is to show your line. Wearing leg warmers, baggy pants, or a loose-fitting sweatshirt will only raise questions about what you're trying to hide.

Finding a Photographer

The best way to obtain exceptional photos is to have them professionally done in a studio. There the photographer can manipulate lighting and background to create a striking image of you—an image that will pay off in the long run. The objective is to acquire professional-looking shots because better print quality will enhance the overall appearance of your résumé package. However, there are ways to achieve these results without spending much money. Call the art department of a nearby university and ask them to recommend a student who might be interested in doing a small job for experience. Sometimes even a professional photographer will do it for free or only charge you the cost of film and developing for a chance to work with a dancer or in hopes of getting referrals. Don't be surprised if the photographer offers you four 8x10 prints in exchange for modeling in another project.

The photographer should take about one hundred shots to be sure of getting an acceptable photograph. Many of the shots will be unusable for different reasons. Black and white photos are fine, although professionally-done color shots can serve you well.

Motion Shots

Motion shots make phenomenal audition photos, but they are often difficult to capture on film. A motion photo comes to life. It is not posed and contrived, but, rather an expression of who you are as a dancer.

Catlin Kirschenbaum   *Photo by: Rosalie O'Connor*

Simple Poses are fine for students and pre-professionals

For jump shots, help the photographer by counting the rhythm of the preparation, and have him or her expose the film on the count on which you intend to strike your pose. This works very well because if the photographer waits to see you in the air, he or she will often catch only the descent and not the explosive part of the jump. In any case, have the photographer take at least twenty shots of each jump to guarantee a usable photo. A dancer arching across the photo in an off-center pull-off creates the image of motion, and these sort of moves can produce impressive images. Even ballet dancers can get away with these off-your-leg shots as long as the photo shows the complete line of the leg and is done in a neo-classical context. By implying motion, the photograph takes on life. Motion is exciting and interesting in a photo.

Stationary Shots

Showing off line in a stationary position also has its advantages. It is easier to obtain satisfactory results if there is time to correct the subtleties of the chosen position. A perfect arabesque is magical, but many arabesques have fallen short of casting their spell due to a misplaced hand or an incorrect focus. Take at least twenty shots of the positions you intend to use, but still be sure to have extra back-up shots of other positions just in case.

Look at a contact sheet and select the three best body shots and the three best face shots and have them blown up to 8x10 for the final selection. A shot that looks good on a contact sheet can be quite scary in 8x10. Ask people which photo is better and judge for yourself.

To reproduce the photos, try having them photocopied at a photocopy service. The technology today is amazing and can produce usable results in both color and black-and- white. Photocopies are inexpensive so consider them if you intend to audition in many places. There are copy services which specialize in quantity and can run off a hundred copies amazingly cheaply compared to having that many

Catlin Kirschenbaum　　　　　　　*Photo by: Rosalie O'Connor*

If you have excellent line and technique like this – show it

printed. With a state-of-the-art copy machine the difference in quality is small.

With a little imagination, the photocopy services can also help you introduce innovation to a résumé package. One dancer taped a color 4x5 dance photo to a piece of paper with his name, address, and phone number laser printed on it. He then had it photocopied, and ended up with an inexpensive, self-marketing flyer which gave his résumé package a unique, professional feel. He also put his name on his head shot by using the same technique.

Hope is the dream of the waking man

FRENCH PROVERB

Chapter 10

Video and DVD

First say to yourself what you would be;
and then do what you have to do .
EPICTETUS

Once, the novelty of receiving a résumé package that included a video was enough to help any dancer stand out above the rest. These days, dance companies routinely use audition videos to pre-screen talent, so it pays to create a video that has impact. "I tend to make up my mind pretty fast," says Anthony Randazzo, a ballet master at Boston Ballet who screens videos. "Sometimes I have a stack of them to watch, so it really helps when a dancer gets to the point. I will use the fast forward button." In researching an article for Dance Magazine, I talked to dance professionals who see mountains of videos every year, and they shared their tips on making a winning tape.

How long should it be? Everyone agrees that audition videos should run between five and 15 minutes. "The first impression happens in a fraction of a second," says Randazzo. "Sometimes I just give a glance at the screen." Make sure only your best images make the video editing cut.

What should you wear? Wear tidy, body-hugging outfits that don't blend into the background. If the floor is black, don't wear black tights because your legs won't show up. If the wall is white, don't wear a white shirt. As for leg warmers, sweats, or a skirt, "Leave them in the dance bag," says William Whitener, artistic director of Kansas City Ballet. "A practice tutu for a classical variation is fine but not necessary."

How about your hair? Hair should be well-groomed. It should be pulled back for ballet women, and for modern, jazz or hip hop, at least partially pulled back. Your hair should never hide your face or be distracting to the viewer. Use good judgment.

Should you say something at the Start? There is nothing wrong with saying your name, location, why you want to dance with the company, and what you're about to perform. Speaking can help make a positive impression. However, be brief. This portion of the video can be filmed in close-up. "It might help register the dancer in the viewer's memory more than a wide shot," says Amy Reusch, dance videographer. Look directly at the camera as if you are talking to a friend, and speak clearly.

What kinds of exercises should you include? Most directors want to see you demonstrate some basic dynamics. Ballet dancers should show adagio, turns, petit allegro, and a grand allegro. Contemporary dancers should present three short pieces (sections of a dance or exercises) that show a similar range--slow movement, spins, fast jumps, and big jumps. Students should also demonstrate some barre work. "We like to see both sides of the barre," says Arlene Minkhorst, director of Royal Winnipeg Ballet School's Professional Division, "so we see both legs working." And barre work needn't be long. Students might show four or five quick exercises: plie tendu, fond de jambe, adagio, and grande battement.

What kinds of pieces should you perform? Professional dancers should also dance a variation, perhaps from a well-known ballet like The Sleeping Beauty, or include an excerpt from a stage performance (only if the video quality is good). Carefully select pieces that are well-suited to the company. "We're looking for a level of intelligence," says Brenda Way, artistic director of ODC/San Francisco. "So make sure you research the company and send an appropriate video." Don't send jazzy examples of your personal choreography to American Ballet Theatre, for instance, because you'll only be showing them you don't know what they do. "If you send us something that is outside the boundaries of what we present," says Randazzo, "it might brighten our day, but it won't help you get a job here."

To pas de deux or not to pas de deux? Ballet men absolutely should perform a duet. "We've started asking men to show some basic partnering in auditions. Seeing it on video is definitely helpful," says Randazzo. Showing partnering moves is also advisable for contemporary dancers. "Regardless of gender--man partnering man, woman with woman, woman with man--I like to see how a dancer relates to other people in a duet," says Way.

What shoes should I wear? Professional level ballet women should definitely dance on pointe. Directors of ballet companies want to know you are proficient and strong. Modern dancers may want to show some combinations in bare feet, and others in jazz shoes or dance sneakers.

How to film? Recruit a friend or fellow dancer to film the video. Use a tripod. Adjust the camera at chest level to the dancer or slightly lower. Make sure the dancer's entire body stays in the flame at all times. Make sure there is enough light in the location--daylight from a big window or skylight is best. Beware of windows in the background, you don't want to shoot your dancer against too much backlight. If you have a studio with windows all around, consider shooting at night. At night time, use clamp-on lights from the hardware store to fully illuminate the studio if the regular overhead lights are not sufficient. Remove all clutter from the background--stuff like dance bags, rosin boxes, chairs, posters, towels, pianos, water bottles. Make sure the music source is near the camera's microphone. If you are lucky enough to get a pianist, place the camera's microphone (if it can be removed) under the piano.

This chapter originally appeared in Dance Magazine Feb. 2005 issue and it's reprinted here due to their generosity.

Have no fear of perfection
—You'll never reach it.
SALVADORE DALI

Chapter 11

On-Line Marketing

The way to gain a good reputation,

Is to endeavor to be what you

desire to appear

SOCRATES

On-line marketing can be a helpful addition to your overall exposure and it can be useful for generating income from dance. This includes the use of email and web pages to help you land the good parts and roles. However, the on-line marketing is not always required and it's an addition to, not a replacement for, the other audition materials and strategies.

Who needs a web site?

A web page certainly isn't necessary for dance students. If you are a pre-professional or a professional performer, on the other hand, consider a web site as your centralized repository for publicity information. Every time you perform a new role, you update your web site. Every time there is a review with your name on it, you scan that and upload to your web site. Every time you see a good photo of you, ask the photographer to let you put it on your site (of course, credit them for taking the photo.) If your friends take some video of you busting fresh moves, add another page to your web site.

Upload video to youtube.com or blip.tv and you can make that video appear on your web site by using a special code that they give you when you upload your video. Put your image out there.

Remember to scan news articles and not just link to the news web sites because many news web sites archive the news, redesign their web sites or otherwise make old stories unavailable.

Established performers might also create a page on en.wikipedia.com and list themselves in the dmoz.com opensource web directory or write a journal using a blog application.

Students can have a web site too, although it isn't required, having one can be fun. If you're under eighteen, you should ask your parents if it's okay and ask them what contact information you can put on your web site, if any. I recommend only an email address and, these days, and a big dose of caution and skepticism about people who contact you.

When NOT to use a web site?

Whether you have your own web page or if you're using services like myspace.com or facebook.com to assemble your information, if you're going to use the site to get dancing roles, remember to keep the content of your page relevant to dance. A director might question your judgment if you send them to a myspace page, which links to your friends drinking beer bongs at the sorority's last kegger. Or if your myspace page is all about modeling, the director might question your focus on dance. So just because you have a web site or page, it doesn't mean you should show it to people when you audition for dance roles.

When to use email?

Use email to keep in touch with former associates. Collect the email addresses of your directors, teachers and colleagues when you're at Summer school or your next show. Then send them an update with your new credits and a story of your dancing adventures each year. How often? No one will get mad if you send them a boilerplate update once a year, or once every six months if you're really performing that much. When your email list is more then family and close friends, it's a good idea to put the email addresses in the "BCC" field when you write your email, instead of in the "To:" field. This will hide the list from everybody who gets your email and they won't know who else you wrote to.

Do I Need the Other Stuff?

Ultimately, a URL to your web site is a supplement to, and not a replacement for, all those other the other parts of your audition message. So even though you have a fantastic web site and the director's email, you still have to send them something that lands on their desk, a hard copy of your résumé on fabulous paper, a printed glossy photo, a timely well written cover letter and, possibly, a DVD.

When you put yourself onto the internet, you still have to put yourself into real world. They're not looking for you in cyberspace – you must grab their attention with the physical material.

Silence does not always mark wisdom
SAMUEL TAYLOR COLERIDGE

Chapter 12

Image and Design

Always bear in mind that your
own resolution to success is more important
than any other one thing
ABRAHAM LINCOLN

A résumé is an advertisement, and as research has shown, an advertisement has only a few seconds to catch a reader's eye. For this reason, simplicity, impact, presentation, readability, and design must be considered to create a job-winning résumé package. Now that you have all the information about yourself and the target company, it is time to mold that information into a professional, high-impact, self-marketing résumé.

Résumé Length

Most dancers can—and should—limit their résumé to one page. As noted earlier, the more professional experience a dancer gains, the less important earlier amateur experience becomes. Although dance companies in Europe and Australia are accustomed to receiving a Curriculum Vitae, which is a complete listing of dance experience, it is unlikely that these epics are often read completely or with interest. Why would a busy director of a respected company care if a new principal dancer once clogged in the French-English friendship pavilion at the Red River Festival back in 1979? Omit this sort of information, to highlight other, more spectacular achievements and still keep a résumé to a readable one page. However, move on to a second page if your work experience truly requires more space to be fairly represented. What is best is what works best for you. If your résumé is already concise but still doesn't fit on one page, don't leave out important facts to squeeze it down. Bear in mind, directors have limited time. They appreciate résumés that avoid long, irrelevant information and communicate the most important facts quickly. If you must add a second page, use a separate piece of paper and staple it to the first. Never print it on the back of the first page.

The main logic behind limiting your résumé to one page is that it enhances clarity. On subsequent pages one can list highlights of newspaper reviews and references.

White Space

White space is the margins and spacing between paragraphs. White space reduces reader fatigue and makes your résumé easier to read because a résumé is more attractive if it has plenty of white space throughout the page. Three-quarter- inch to one-inch margins are standard for a résumé. Look at the bad example résumé to see what happens if there is no white space.

Proofreading

Bad grammar and misspelled words on a résumé turn off an employer. The director is forced to wonder how a person who cares so little about a résumé will present himself or herself on stage. Check spelling of all the people and choreography on your résumé because one of the names you misspell might be a friend of the director or his or her favorite ballet. Check all dates, your address, and phone number. Read the cover letter and résumé once for spelling, once for punctuation and capitalization, and then read it backwards to catch the mistakes you missed. Finally, have someone else proofread.

Fonts and Sizes

There are many advantages to using a computer to write your résumé. If you don't have continued access to one, don't overlook secretarial and word processing services. Also many photocopy shops have résumé services. Such a service can key a résumé onto computer disk, and from there corrections are easy, cheap, and fast. By having your résumé on disk, you can easily format your résumé to accommodate different target companies and add to the disk as you gain more experience.

Part of the design of a résumé and cover letter is created by the choice of font. A font is the style of lettering and the size is, of course, the size of the letter.

Use a serif font. A serif font has the little platforms and hooks the top and the bottom of each letter. Virtually every newspaper and book is written in a serif font because they are easy to read. Definitely write your cover letter in a serif font.

Sans serif literally means "without serif." These fonts are less conservative and a bit harder to read so don't use them on your cover letter. Sans serif fonts are acceptable for a dance résumé.

Use only one or two different fonts on your résumé. More fonts detract from the design and readability, creating a visual font-salad, which isn't appealing, unless you're making an advertisement for Wired Magazine.

Instead of using an additional font, key elements of a résumé can be highlighted by underlining, using italics, or printing boldly. Use these frills sparingly, however, because they tend to lose their impact if overused. Also avoid using all three at the same time.

Paper

Résumés and cover letters are most effective when printed on matching paper. Photocopy shops and stationary stores stock all kinds of paper. Eight-and-a-half by eleven inch, 25-pound bond paper in buff, cream, pale gray, and light brown are good choices. When selecting paper color, remember that your résumé is not modern art. Let your art be dancing, and select a color that looks sophisticated, professional, and unassuming. Consider heavier weight paper which gives a crisp-feeling résumé.

Fancy Folders

After putting so much effort into assembling your audition package, it's nice to display it in a folder or pouch. Many report folders are available in office and art supply stores. Find one that works for you. Some have clear covers which can create a nice effect if you let one of your photos show through. Others have a slot for a business card, if you have one, and this also creates a professional impression.

Some folders have "made from recycled paper" discreetly printed on the back. This might be a subtle way to indicate your environmental thoughtfulness. If the director you target is involved in the recycling movement, this sort of prudent self-marketing can be effective.

Word of Warning!

Many dancers go overboard in a desperate attempt to make their résumé unique. It's all been done. People have lied, cheated, and sent singing telegrams. People have printed their résumés on T-shirts, in books, used leather folders, printed color brochures, sent nude photos, and even mailed computer multi-media disks. One résumé appeared on a billboard in Los Angels. People have sent oversized résumés with poster-sized face shots. One aspiring ballerina sent her point shoe in a box with a letter reading, "Now that I've got my foot in the door, how about an audition?"

DO NOT try any of these methods! Only consider such revolutionary methods if you are familiar with, or have researched, your target company, and are SURE your efforts will be appreciated. The dance world is small and people talk. Your reputation is on the line. Generally, directors want a conservative and professional-looking résumé. Many are skeptical of extremely unusual approaches.

It is true that some directors are certainly looking for unusual and creative dancers who will "go the extra mile" to get noticed. These directors are far and few between, however, and it is wiser to try a radical approach only if it is based on intimate knowledge of the director or an uncanny insight to human nature.

Let us train our minds to
desire what the situation demands.
SENECA
4 B.C.—65 A.D.

Chapter 13

Securing an Audition

They always say that time
changes things, but you
actually have to change
them yourself.
ANDY WARHOL

The Cattle Call

When a company needs dancers they schedule an audition. Many major dance companies hold their auditions once a year in New York City. These auditions have earned the dubious title of "cattle calls" because of their resemblance to the meat-processing industry. Hundreds of dancers are herded into a room as cows are herded onto the auction block. Only unlike the cows, the dancers are sometimes required to pay a small fee for being there. Because of the sheer volume of auditioners, cattle calls are often unsuccessful for all involved. Dancers have trouble being noticed in the crowd, and directors don't have the time to properly evaluate each dancer's talent.

One disadvantage of a cattle call audition is that some directors ask for a dancer's résumé only after the audition is over. The director then collects only the résumés of those dancers with whom he or she is interested. To minimize this disadvantage, send your résumé to the director about a week before the scheduled audition. Mention in your cover letter that you will see the director at the audition; then bring additional copies of your résumé and photos to the audition.

Research for this book revealed that some directors, like Eliot Feld, have their own "employer's questionnaire" and don't require a résumé at all. Only after judging a dancer as a possible employee will he examine the results of that dancer's questionnaire. Luckily for the self-marketing dancer, directors who use these methods are the exception rather than the rule. Sending your résumé in advance can't hurt, even if your research identified such a director.

Some larger ballet companies such as ABT, New York City Ballet, and San Francisco Ballet (to name a few), like to see a letter of introduction and recommendation from an established school, teacher, other ballet company, or former alumnus, particularly in the case of a new, young dancer who has not been formerly associated with a professional ballet company. Such a letter is also valuable when auditioning for smaller companies.

Audition by Invitation

Most companies prefer to audition dancers in the general scheduled auditions but will see dancers by invitation in company class. To secure an invitation, send a résumé, cover letter, and photos directly to the artistic director. Write "Audition Materials Enclosed" on the outside of the envelope to insure the résumé package arrives on the proper desk. If interested, the director will invite the dancer to do class.

Always try to get an invitation before going to the scheduled audition. Making an appointment for a private audition improves your chances of winning a job considerably. Private auditions are simply less chaotic.

Call the director's assistant, about four or five business days after sending the résumé, to make sure they got the package, and to confirm an appointment. If the director's assistant says that they need time to decide, ask when you may call back. Many circumstances prevent a director from responding to a résumé. He or she might be out of town or otherwise unavailable. Therefore, if you get a "don't call us-we'll call you" response—don't despair. Sometimes a director really does want to wait before granting an audition.

If they say there are no positions available, ask when they will know if a contract is opening up. The key is to be persistent—but don't be a pest! Be very sensitive to the person's tone of voice for signals of annoyance while talking on the phone. As a rule, don't call more then once a week—once every two weeks is better.

If you are traveling to a city and want to audition for the local company, always arrange for the audition beforehand. Your chances of being seen by the proper people are increased if they know you are coming. Furthermore, it is polite to call before you show up at the door.

It is a general policy among dance companies not to pay for any expenses incurred by an auditioner while seeking a job. Knowing this, many directors are reluctant to grant an audition to a dancer if there are no available positions in the company's roster. Yet the same director might jump and make room in the company if he or she saw the dancer in action. It's a Catch 22 of Terpsichore. Try relieving the director's conscience enough to grant you an audition appointment by mentioning in your cover letter that you are traveling to the city anyway (to see friends or family) and wish to take this time to audition. In such a case, keep the exact dates of your "family visit" unclear, as in, "I will be traveling to Los Angeles in March to visit my sister and wonder if it is convenient for Mr. Jenson to see me in class at that time." If Mr. Jenson is available on the 30th then visit your "sister" late in the month.

On the other hand, a company might pay for your audition expenses if they are interested enough in you, are desperate to fill a position, or need a partner for a ballerina. Just because they might pay doesn't mean they will offer, so it does not hurt to ask.

Every ceiling, when reached, becomes

a floor, upon which one walks as a matter

of course and prescriptive right.

ALDOUS HUXLEY

Chapter 14

Fear and the Audition

Courage is grace under pressure.
ERNEST HEMINGWAY

Understand that the résumé, photos, and cover letter are only a prelude to the audition. It is in the audition where hard work and dedication pay off big. Yes, it is possible—and important—to create a fantastic first impression with a résumé, but no one will hire a dancer from a résumé alone. This requires a successful audition.

The Fear of Failure

It takes courage to face an audition. Dancers are never more vulnerable and exposed than they are at the moment when they show their body and art in a struggle for employment. In the audition, your hopes and dreams are completely in the hands of others. With a nod from the director, your dreams are either realized, or if the director is unimpressed, go unfulfilled. Dancers, even more than other artists, find it particularly hard to take criticism because it's easy for dancers to perceive their art as themselves. "We don't like your dancing" feels like "We don't like you" because the separation of you and your dancing is rarely obvious.

Yet the auditioning is a never-ending necessity in the dance world. Even a member of a major professional company, and a dancer for many years, faces auditions throughout the season and the possibility of rejection on a daily basis. Nevertheless, each dancer finds the courage and the strength to continue.

To be a dancer, one must audition. Every dancer faces this struggle and each must develop a unique and personal way of managing to continue in spite of it. How you deal with your fears at an audition can mean the difference between being a professional dancer or wishing you were.

The fear of failure is one of the most intense fears anyone can experience. Many people are so afraid of failing they simply avoid situations that might bring out the crippling emotion. They stop trying, or they just try a little bit, so when they fail they can say, "Well, I wasn't really trying."

Other people cope with the fear by denying it altogether. This is dangerous because when an emotion is denied it's only amplified. An auditioning dancer might succeed in denying his or her fear—until the director walks into class. Then all the fear that's been hidden will suddenly rush forth with a force that can be paralyzing.

The Fear of Rejection

By auditioning, you have invited someone to tell you either "Yes, I like your dancing enough to accept you" or "No, your dancing is not good enough." In addition to the fear of failure, a dancer must face the fear of rejection. For many, these emotions are overwhelming, and can devastate an audition performance. For others, these emotions have a creeping effect that only unnerves the dancer just enough to sabotage the audition class. Yet for some, the fear of failure and rejection has no negative consequence. How do some dancers give a peak performance in spite of their emotions? How can you?

Label the feeling of fear as excitement. From now on, call the anxiety, the churning stomach, and the copper taste of fear by its new name—excitement. It sounds easy because it is. One of the greatest discoveries of the Twentieth Century is the realization that human beings can alter their lives by altering their mental attitudes. Put another way: You can change how you feel. The feeling you experience when you are about to audition is a gift from the primitive times when humans were still commanded by fight- or-flight instincts. But you can not fight or flee from your auditions and expect to be a dancer. Instead, use the energy that accompanies fear to work harder, focus more, and stand taller. Realize that it takes great courage to face an audition, and by simply trying your hardest, or at least learning something from the experience, you have succeeded.

The Fear of Success

Success brings changes. You may have to work late or perhaps move to another city. A new job means added responsibility. Winning a job can also change your routine. The fear of change can manifest as the fear of success. Arrest this culprit by first clearly writing out your goals in dance, secondly, deciding you absolutely need this job to reach your dance goals and, finally, come to terms with each change your new job will bring.

Losers visualize the penalties of failure.
Winners visualize the rewards of success.
DR. ROB GILBERT

Focus on the positive changes and come to terms with the negative changes. If getting a job means moving away from your current boyfriend, you have to accept this reality before you can truly give your best effort.

Your Best Equals Success

Successful dancers combat their fear by trying their hardest. Fear becomes their excitement, which puts them into a powerful state and motivates them do their best. By doing their best, these dancers realize they have succeeded, regardless of what others think. Furthermore, they realize that doing their best starts long before the actual audition. You must do your best before, during, and after class. This means doing workouts in addition to dance class and stretching, avoiding the habit of eating junk foods, and taking the time and care to prepare a professional-looking résumé package. It is a great help to know that, at least on paper, you look the absolute best you can. A outstanding résumé will help you to resist the fear of an audition and is therefore essential to your confidence.

A dancer who is rehearsed and ready for a performance experiences less stage fright. For the same reason, a brilliant résumé will give you confidence when it is time to audition. Begin easing the anxiety of audition early by preparing an excellent résumé today. Besides, directors enjoy watching an audition with a clear, persuasive, and professional-looking résumé in front of them.

Don't underestimate this advantage. The dance world is a business. When you ask for a job, you must show that you are a serious professional or intend to become one. Set yourself apart from the thousands of "flakes" who call themselves dancers.

Never let the fear of striking out

get in your way.

GEORGE HERMAN "BABE" RUTH

Chapter 15

Last Thoughts Before Your Audition

Courage is grace under pressure.
ERNEST HEMINGWAY

Never be late for an audition! Always leave time for: Traffic jams, Late busses, Broken alarm clocks, a car that won't start, blizzards, earthquakes, acts of terrorism -- whatever -- don't be late. (remember, American Ballet Theater performed on the evening of September 11th, 2001! The show goes on...)

Also, if you start to get nervous before or at your audition, remember that fear is excitement. Excitement is good! You must thrive on this energy. Other dancers at the audition might appear better then you, but they may not be what the director is seeking. Do not be intimidated by them.

A good director understands that you may be nervous, especially if you are young and inexperienced. He or she may try to put you at ease with a smile or a correction, but don't rely on that. Some directors may actually get pleasure from intimidation you with difficult exercises or by giving you a long stare just to see how you dance under pressure. Give each moment your best effort, and as long as you are trying your best, then that's all you can do -- right? And Always maintain eye contact, even while dancing, do show the director what you are mad of. Maintain concentration and understand the coordination of the exercise before you begin -- even if it means going with a second or third group.

Retain your composure. Remember that the director had to audition when he or she was a dancer. The more at ease you are, the more at ease the director will be while watching you dance.

Visualize a successful audition. See it as a positive experience. It is your rendezvous with destiny--a journey of discovery.

Do not stretch on the floor while everyone else is marking the combinations. Dance the combinations exactly as given. Sometimes it only irritates a director if you try impressing him or her with extra pirouettes or beats.

If you try your hardest and the director seams uninterested, ignores you, or doesn't see you after class, don't let it bother you. Find a better person to work for, one who extends the respect you deserve.

Always be polite -- with the secretary, with the dancers, with everyone. Be courteous on the phone and in person. These people may soon be your colleagues. Keep a positive mental attitude, a superior techniques, and a winning attitude. You have a brilliant résumé -- so be brilliant!

> *It's all right to have butterflies*
> *in your stomach. Just get*
> *them to fly in formation.*
> **DR. ROB GILBERT**

Chapter 16

Case Studies and Sample Résumés

I will not steep my speech
In lies; the test of any man
Lies in action.
PINDAR
522-433 B.C.

About This Chapter

The sample résumés are here so you may compare their formats and imitate their styles. Three case studies, each with a detailed commentary about the résumés, cover letters, and rest of the audition package begin, followed by some sample résumés with comments hand-written on them. Finally, there is a short commentary on the two "bad examples" and one "bad cover letter."

All the names, addresses, and events in the following résumés and cover letters are fabricated, with no intended similarities to or relationship with people living or dead. The events, dates, addresses, and phone numbers appearing on the résumés are fictional. Some of the classic choreographic works and names of noted choreographers are included on the résumés unchanged to add clarity and points of reference to the samples. However, it is not the intention of the author to harm anyone's reputation or invade anyone's privacy.

You are permitted to copy short sections of this book for your résumé or cover letter with out violation the copyright law or without being liable for plagiarism.

Case Study 1: Jennifer Rosestein

Jennifer uses the functional format because of her recent changes in dance schools and her limited performing experience. She spent the past two years alternating between Ballet West summer school in Aspen, San Francisco Ballet summer school, North Carolina School of the Arts, Jacops Pillow, and Rainbow Dance Academy in Telluride. Furthermore, she has very little performing experience. All her performing experience is included on her résumé, other then appearing as a ladybug at the Annual Summer Solstice Fair in Telluride. (She wisely chose the functional format over the chronological because her frequent changes in training, as well as limited performing experience, would have been highlighted by a chronological format.

A great physique for ballet, noted motivation, and a generally positive attitude are in Jennifer's favor. The functional format permits her to mention these qualities eloquently. She uses the magic word "promises."

Jennifer decides to write about herself in the third person because it sounds very confident and factual. The effect is that the text appears to have been written by someone else or even quoted from a newspaper review—a very professional look.

She mentions she is from Colorado in the Education section, instead of indicating citizenship at the top of her résumé beneath the date of birth, height, and weight.

Jennifer includes references directly on her résumé, knowing that Sandra Johnson and Ruth Stenn are acquaintances of Ms. Koma, the artistic director of Ballet East. Furthermore, she is sure they will each give and hones opinion of her level. She contacts all three references before sending the résumé package, fills them in on her recent activities, and mentions Ms. Koma might call and ask about her.

Jennifer looks great on her résumé in spite of her limited experience. Furthermore, Ms. Koma was pleased to notice Jennifer is willing to take an apprentice contract if no *corps de ballet* contracts are available. She found this personalized résumé easy to read and intriguing.

Her cover letter is excellent. It follows the standards and advice outlined in Chapter 8 and clearly states her objective in a very flattering manner.

A professional photographer took her photos in exchange for modeling in another project. So they were inexpensive and look great.

She displays the material in a sleek, black folder with the cover letter on the outside where it will be seen first. Unfortunately, Jennifer let the photocopy shop use their standard copy paper, which is poor quality bond and detracts from the condition of her otherwise excellent audition package.

Jennifer Rosestein
1735 Washington St.
Houston, TX 64115
February 6, 1994

Ms. Blanca Roma, Artistic Director
Ballet East
50 West 200 South
Portland, UT 84101

Dear Ms. Roma:

It has been a special joy of mine to watch Ballet East position itself as one of the top ballet companies in America. Furthermore, it has been a long-time dream of mine to dance in your company, and I am finally ready to submit my résumé for your review.

While a scholarship student at North Carolina School of the Arts, I worked hard and focused on my ballet training so that I might realize my dream of being a member of Ballet East. The effort paid off when the staff at North Carolina selected me to open the production of Act II-La Bayadère as Nikiya.

I have been dancing for ten years and feel I am ready to take an entry level position in a major ballet company.

I will be traveling to Portland to visit my brother in March, and if it is convenient for you, it would be my privilege to be seen at that time. I will call your assistant in one week to confirm an appointment.

Thank you for your consideration.

Sincerely yours,

Jennifer Rosestein

Jennifer Rosestein

Enclosure

Jennifer Rosestein

1735 Washington St.
Houston, TX 64115
(415) 763-1992

Birth Date. - May 8, 1977
Height - 5'6"
Weight - 116 lbs.

Objective: Entry position in Ballet East.

Featured roles:
- Featured as Nikiya in La Bayadère while on scholarship for North Carolina School of the Arts.

- Appeared as Tea in Raleigh Ballet's production of The Nutcracker.

- Danced in an ensemble for San Francisco Ballet School's end-of-the-year production.

Education: Jennifer Rosestein is from Telluride, Colorado, and started dancing at the Rainbow Dance Academy. She received additional training at the North Carolina School of the Arts as a scholarship student, the San Francisco Ballet summer school, Ballet West summer school and at Jacops Pillow.

Jennifer is a dancer with a great physique. She possesses an explosive jump, confident turns, and brilliant beats. Jennifer is very quick at picking up new choreography and promises to become a fine professional dancer.

References:

George Thorn
821 W. 51st. St.
New York, NY 00987
(212) 643-3890

Sandra Johnson
321 Main St.
Telluride, CO 31244
(301) 432-1219

Ruth Stenn
455 Banklin St.
Oakland, CA 33190
(415) 546-9287

Case Study Two: Richard Lewis and Janis Welmond

Mr. Lewis is action as an agent. Janis Welmond and himself have made the effort to format their audition package to a singular style to market them as a dancing team. The entire package includes two résumés, one cover letter, two sheets of quotations from newspaper reviews (Mr. Lewis's sheet is not shown), eight photos, and one DVD of the couple dancing in various performances. It was mailed to eighteen different companies, with minor changes to the cover letter, of course, at a total cost of $289.98. However, the nine performances secured from this marketing investment yielded $16,500—enough to justify the expense.

Mr. Lewis places his experience with Markarova at the top of his résumé even though ten years have passed since they danced in Mexico City. He was in the *corp de ballet* of The National Ballet of Canada when he danced *Five Tangos* by Hans Van Manen. In this ballet there is a moment when each *corps* boy partners the lead lady for about eight seconds. This is the extent of his experience with Markarova, but Mr. Lewis feels having partnered such a famous ballerina generates interest in his résumé. He omits the detail of dancing in the *corp* and not as "her partner" because he is a self-marketer who wants this guesting job and because he never mentions negative information on his résumé.

They use chronological format because of the conservative image it projects. Furthermore, Mr. Lewis likes the way it demonstrates the natural progression of his career—from the moment he began dancing in his parents' ballet studio in 1969, all the way to his present principal contract. His résumé quickly shows his "rise to the top" in a subtle yet progressive manner.

Missing from his résumé are the roles he danced as a student and apprentice. In addition, he only lists the soloist roles he danced while in the *corp de ballet*, and only the principal roles he danced as a soloist. This gives the impression that Mr. Lewis is somewhat of a prodigy.

Mr. Lewis also doesn't list the many demi-soloist and character roles he has been dancing for the past few years in Boston. Indeed, this would hint at the reason he is seeking employment elsewhere. Many of his recent roles would detract from the image of a leading classical dancer.

Mr. Lewis and Ms. Welmond have no shortage of roles to put on their résumés. If they wished, they could fill up three pages of professional experience. Instead, they wisely include only their greatest and most classical performances.

Mr. Lewis has their résumés on computer disk so he may easily alter them to suit each new target company or career goal. Furthermore, he has all correspondence proofread and copy-edited from a professional editorial service he found on-line. This always insures a professional writing style.

If you have demonstrated a box office draw as Ms. Welmond has, be sure to highlight it on your résumé.

In composition, the focal point of a page is about one third from the top. The focal point on a résumé is right where you summary of experience or career highlights goes. Your eye naturally travels to this focal point, where Mr. Lewis mentions his experience with a great Ballerina, and Ms. Welmond mentions her noted popularity with the public. Position your most interesting experience on the focal point of your résumé.

Richard Lewis
6314 Starlight Lane
Boston, MA 64109
September 12, 1994

Mr. Marcus Washington, Artistic Director
Ballet Freedom
543 Washington Drive
Denver, CO 77603

Dear Mr. Washington:

I am writing on behalf of myself and my partner, Janis Welmond, to express our interest in performing as guest artists in your production of The Nutcracker. Review of the enclosed résumé will reveal that I have been a member of your former company, The National Ballet of Canada, and it is based on your reputation there that I became interested in working with you.

As principal dancers at Boston Ballet, Janis and I have worked together in some exciting roles. Furthermore, we have performed as guest artists extensively. Our experience together include:

- Performed *Stars and Stripes* pas de deux by invitation at Ballet British Columbia's Gala.

- Received impassioned reviews as opening night lead couple for *Swan Lake* in Boston.

- Featured in *Tchaikovsky Pas de deux* in an eight-week tour of Europe which was billed as "Stars of the Ballet."

In addition to dancing together for several years, we have been presented on the cover of the Feburary 1991 issue of Dance Magizine and in two separate advertisement campaigns for Ballet Boston. This sort of publicity could mean added ticket sales for your Nutcracker.

Should you feel that we can contribute to your production, I would welcome the opportunity arrange a meeting. I can be reached at (204) 352-1108.

Thank you for your consideration.

Sincerely,

Richard Lewis

Enclosure

Janis Welmond

"Possessing a slender, seemingly boneless body, she rode the crest of Tchaikovsky's music with such a powerful lyrical impulse that the effect was to give visual form to pure emotion."
William Littler
The Toronto Star
May 8, 1988

"...moves with a sort of grave self-absorption as if she were simply the instrument of dance...she has the ineffable image of greatness about her."
Clive Barnes
New York Post
June 8, 1992

"Gripping, absolutely hypnotizing; Miss Soulen's performance as Lizzy Borden had me rivoted to my seat."
Judas Free
Dancepress
October 26, 1994

Richard Lewis

6314 Starlight Lane
Boston, MA 64109
Home: 310-456-0798
Fax: 310-456-0789

Height: 6' 1"
Weight: 161 lbs.
Date of Birth: March 19, 1962
Citizenship: Canadian
Visa: Workers Permit

Objective:

To dance Nutcracker's grand pas de deux and variation as a guest artist, with partner Janis Welmond, for an American regional ballet company.

Summary of Experience:

- Partnered Makarova in *Five Tangos* (Van Manen) with Bellas Artes in Mexico City.

- Featured roles include Prince Desire in *The Sleeping Beauty*, Prince Siegfried in *Swan Lake* (Goredonivech), principal roles in *The Four Temperaments*, the first movement of *Symphony in C*, and *Ballo della Regina* (Balanchine), Head Wrangler in *Rodeo* (de Mille).

- Enjoyed success dancing *Stars and Stripes* pas de deux (Balanchine) by invitation with Janis Welmond at Ballet British Columbia's Gala and as a guest artist with the National Ballet of Canada in *Alice* (Tetley).

Professional Experience:

Principal - Ballet Boston   1990 - Present
Other Featured roles include: Colas in *La Fille Mal Gardee* (Ashton) Cavalier in *Nutcracker* and *Black Swan* pas de deux (Petipa).
Soloist - Basil Ballet   1986 - 1990
Featured as principal male in *Études* (Lander), and *Tchaikovsky pas de deux* (Balanchine).
Corps de Ballet - The National Ballet of Canada   1982 - 1986
Danced pas de six in *Napoli* (Schaufuss) and other corps roles.
Apprentice - The National Ballet School   1980 - 1982
Hired immediately upon graduation from The National Ballet School.

Education:

Scholarship student for the National Ballet School   1976 - 1980
Attended the Boston Ballet Summer School   1975
Studied ballet, tap, jazz, modern, and ballroom   1967 - 1975
dance at parents' ballet school in Ontario, Canada.

A Guide to Self-Marketing for Performers

Janis Welmond
343-8th Avenue
Boston, MA 54490
310-548-0098

Height: 5' 6"
Weight: 115 lbs.
Date of Birth: May 16, 1967
Citizenship: British

Objective:

To dance Nutcracker's grand pas de deux and variation as a guest artist, with partner Richard Lewis, for an American regional ballet company.

Summary of Experience:

- Demonstrated her ability as a box office draw for Ballet Boston.

- Featured in the leading roles in *Agon*, the first movement of *Symphony in C, Stars and Stripes, Who Cares?, Bugaku, Apollo,* and *Serenade* (Balanchine)

- Recieved standing ovations after performing Odette/Odeal in *Swan Lake* (Mc Marlin), Juliet in *Romeo and Juliet* (Kerchanko), Giselle in *Giselle* (Suiter), Nikiya in *La Bayadére* (Karinski), and Titania in *A Midsummers Night's Dream.*

Professional Experience:

Pricipal - Ballet Boston   1989 - Present
Other featured roles include: The Ecstasy of Mary Windston (Remond), On the Top Somewhat in the Middle (Sythner), and The Bloody Pavan (Kinsmore.)
Soloist - Ballet Boston   1988 - 1989
Featured as an emerging star in Ballet Boston's *Giselle* (Suiter.)
Corps de ballet - Ballet Boston   1986 -1988
Performed Odette/Odeal in *Swan Lake* (Mc Marlin) and the Sugar Plum Fairy in *Nutcracker* (Russ) while still in the corp.

Education:

Graduate with honors from the New York City American Ballet School. Studied for eight years on full scholarship in this prestigious program.

Awards:

Gold medalist in the 1992 Berlin International Ballet Competition.

Case Study Three: Wendy Mathews

Wendy uses two different résumés and considers each a self-marketing tool. She is the type of dancer who sees what she wants and then takes it. She constantly updates, revises, and personalizes her résumés to maximize their effectiveness and fit the situation.

She has used both a chronological and functional résumé this year for many special instances.

She secured work by submitting the chronological résumé to Rachel White and Fred Robinson while on layoff from Collective Dance. Wendy knows both of them personally and even spent some time at their house during a reception. Furthermore, she is sure they watched her perform as a member of Collective Dance. In spite of this, Wendy knows a résumé is essential for a professional relationship so she keeps the greeting formal. Understanding both Mr. Robson and Ms. White are great fans of Collective Dance, Wendy devoted much of this résumé to her experience there. In addition, Ms. White has recently used African rhythm in recent dance piece, which is reason enough to give her studies in African a heading of it's own.

She uses the functional résumé three different times this year in application for a grant, as a résumé for teaching job, and as a public relations biography for an article in *Rock and Ice*. She wrote the grant to gain funding to study the new concept of dancing on a wall using a climbing harness and rope. *Rock and Ice* wanted to know more about her dance career so she sent them the functional version. She also used this in a pinch when the University of South Arizona asked for a bio prior to her teaching there in the summer. The request came at a moment when Wendy was very busy so she was glad that she had this version of her résumé to quickly use as a publicity statement. She simply removed the last paragraph about rock climbing and wrote in more about her other teaching experience. For the grant application, the rock climbing publicity statement and the teaching biography, there was no need to include her height, weight or age.

Other Example Résumés

Following Wendy's résumés are five additional résumés, which use some hybrid variation of functional and chronological format. Notice the good use of white space and the clear clean presentation.

> *It is hard to fail, but it is worse*
> *never to have tried to succeed.*
> **THEODORE ROOSEVELT**

<u>W E N D Y   M A T H E W S</u>

534 Assinaboin Ave.
Calgary, Alberta J3B-3H4
Canada
(204) 756-9304

Date of Birth: January 30, 1967   Height: 5'5"
Citizenship: American and Canadian   Weight: 115 lbs.

EXPERIENCE:
Eight years of professional performing experience as both a solo performer and as a part of three dance ensembles. Worked closely with Paul Taylor in the creation of *Roses* and *Last Look*.

Founding member of Collective Dance, a progressive movement company founded in 1991. Due to the driven work ethic and magical talent of the director, Joyce Joplyn, Collective Dance enjoyed impassioned reviews and phenomenal success.

CAREER BACKGROUND:

COLLECTIVE DANCE   1991-Present
Featured dancer and guest choreographer. Worked with Joyce Joplyn as her "choreographic tool" and was involved in every process of production. Responsible for, as a member of this unique company:
— Set and costume design for three major productions.
— Public relations and press release manager.
— Complete marketing of performances.

CANADA COUNCIL GRANT   1990-1991
Wrote and won $18,000 grant from the Canada Council. Traveled to Africa to study the rhythms and movements of the African Swahili.

PAUL TAYLOR COMPANY   1986-1990
Featured in both *Roses* and *Last Look* on CBS For the Arts. Also appeared in *Request, Alto and Tenor*, and *Give Away*.

EDUCATION:

THE JULLARD SCHOOL   1982-1986
Bachelor of Fine Arts degree — Received training in the styles of Martha Graham, Jose Limon, Eric Hawkins and Merce Cunningham.

ALBERTA SCHOOL   1977-1982
OF CONTEMPORARY DANCE
Determined and motivated student at this respected professional school.

WENDY MATHEWS

543 Assinaboin Avenue
Calgary, Alberta J3B-3H4
Canada
(204) 756-9304

For the past three years I have been a member of the Calgary-based modern dance company COLLECTIVE DANCE. In addition to the regular performances during the season in Calgary, we toured to The Performing Arts Center at SUNY Purchase in New York, the Dancing-On-The-Edge Festival in Vancouver, the Yukon Arts Center in Yellow Knife, the Festival of Canadian Modern Dance in Ottawa, and the Du Maurier New Music Festival in Winnipeg. Furthermore, I performed the works of independent choreographers Rachel White, Stephanie Allard, and Fred Robson while on layoff.

I gained much experience dancing with Paul Taylor's Company in New York. As a member of this company for four years, I formed a professional approach to dance and learned so much in Mr. Taylor's tutelage

I received my early dance training under the direction of May Quaker at the Alberta School of Contemporary Dance. Later, after successfully completing all the required courses of the JULIARD dance program, I was awarded a Bachelor of Fine Arts degree. I experienced additional training at Santa Rose State University with Matt Fredrick, Marty Gaston, and Mary Van Wall.

In 1990, I was awarded an $18,000 Canada Council grant to study the rhythms and movement styles of the African Swahili. Throughout my career I have received scholarships, grants, and awards form the Alberta Arts Council to further my artistic development.

As a teacher, I improved my skills by giving class at the Alberta School of Contemporary Dance on a regular basis. In addition, I have taken the opportunity to use the students from the junior and senior divisions to begin development of my own choreographic style.

For the past year and a half I pursued my interest in rock climbing as a component of my dance training and personal expression. I hope in time to discover a new training program for dancers by integrating dance and climbing . Moreover, I feel this insight will enable me to develop a vertical choreographic vocabulary which is unique and distinct.

JOHN THOMSON

5689 Justin Boulevard
Santa Barbra, CA 94109
(415) 563-0883

Height: 1.78 m. (5' 9")
Weight: 70 Kg. (155 lbs)
Nationality: German
DOB: January 20, 1968

Career Highlights:

- Partnered Ekaterina Martina in *L ' Petit Papion* by Roland Grand and danced as Zaza Jeaneriea's partner in a cabaret tour in Europe.

- Demonstrated lead male fineness and ability dancing the pas de deux *Flower Festival at Genzano* by August Bournonville and grand pas de deux in *The Nutcracker* by David Lopez, and used extensively by him as a partner for his principal ballerinas.

- Appeared with Star Dancers Ballet in Tokyo, and danced *Donizetti Variations* by Balanchine as guest artist for Japan Ballet Festival.

Summary of Experience:

Ballet Santa Barbara   1992-1994
Featured as lead male in W. Freeman's *Progress Equals Decay,* in the pas de deux from George Balanchine's *Agon* and his first movement finale of *Symphony in C.* Other lead roles include:
Love is Real by J. Kumeska, *I Da Da Dance* by I. Harrison, *The Fantasy* and *Our Sons* by D. Bender, and several roles by artistic director David Lopez.

Dance Theater of New York   1990-1992
Worked with Glen Letter to create a solo and a pas de deux in *Diapers,* in addition to dancing the pas de deux and pas de trois in his *Volume.* Other featured roles were: *Flower Festival at Genzano* by August Buornonville, *Gary* by B. Wilson, and *Mind Game* by R. South.

Ballet National de Leon   1985-1990
Featured in White Duck variation in *Ma Nijinski* for television broadcast and Arabian Dance of the *Nutcracker* in addition to other roles.

Dance Education:

Conservatoire national superieur
de musique de Paris   1982-1985
Trained by Andrew Ritz and Serge Gostovski, and passed the required music, dance history, and dance theory examinations.

Victoria King

Before September 3, 1994		After September 3, 1994
12512 Saber Lane		118 W. 61st St.
Bowie, Maryland 20945		New York, NY 10023
(989) 345-2998		(212) 488-0198
Height: 5' 4"	**Weight:** 112 lbs.	**D.O.B.** June 4, 1965

Major successes:

♦ Finalist on Ed Mc Mahon's *Star Search* dance competition; created the choreography and was responsible for rehearsing six dancers to a performance level. Danced live on camera for over eight million people.

♦ Guest appearance on *The Love Boat* as a seasick belly dancer, involved in on-location shooting and required to improve a small variation.

♦ Emerging star on Broadway. Featured in *The Carousel*, by Rogers and Hammerstein and received splendid reviews for dancing in *The Ghost Stage* by Liza Frederic.

Experience:

Over fourteen years of professional dance experience stands testament to Victoria's commitment to the art. She has danced in ballet companies, modern dance groups, jazz showcases, and large Hollywood tap numbers.

Victoria has demonstrated her abilities to twenty-three different choreographers as a professional dancer; adapted well to each process and proved herself to be a committed performer.

Paloma Jerez
3789 Polk St.
Cupertino, CA 95110
(417) 234-1109

Height: 5'6"
Weight: **114 lbs.**
D.o.b.: **12/6/74**
Country: **Spain**

Objective:

A job dancing in Canada.

Outstanding achievements:

- Danced principal roles in *Paquita*, *La Bayadére*, and *Grand Pas de Quatre* with Joven Ballet de María de Ávila.

- Performed with the San Francisco Ballet in *The Nutcracker*, *Swan Lake*, and *Symphony in C*.

- Featured in Gala of the Stars in Madrid, sharing the stage with Isabel Guerinm, Wilfried Romoli, Nina Ananiashuili, and Alexie Fadeyechev.

Dance Training:

Apprentice for The San Francisco Ballet	1993-1994
Scholarship student for The San Francisco Ballet	1992-1993
Escuela de danza Mª de Ávila in Zaragoza, Spain. Graduated from the program with "Excellent Qualifications"	1982-1992

Awards:

Received a grant from the Ministerio de Cultura in Spain to complete dance training in a foreign country.

VERONICA WAITE

423 W. 55th St.
New York, NY 10023
212-555-7984

Birth date: 2-1-72
Height: 5'5"
Weight: 97 Lbs.

PROFESSIONAL ACTIVITIES:

- Performed with the San Francisco Ballet in the new production of *The Sleeping Beauty* (Tomasson), *Divertimento* (Tomasson) and in two years of *The Nutcracker* (Christensen).

- Appeared on PBS dancing *Coppelia* and *Metro Dancin'* with the Mainland Ballet Theatre, and was also seen on TV in two commercials advertising ballet.

- Additional performing experience includes *Tomorrow* (La Frick), *Brother Lament* (Red), *Jumpin' Nostalgia* (Tansma), *West Side Story, 42nd Street, Sweet Charity,* and ten years of *The Nutcracker*.

TRAINING:

Currently enrolled in the San Francisco Ballet School and receive daily classes in ballet, modern, pas de deux, dance history, character, and point.

Received extensive ballet training from School of American Ballet, San Francisco Ballet School, Pacific Northwest Ballet School, and the Pennsylvania School of Ballet.

Danced for ten years at the Mero Dance Academy and obtained additional training and performing experience with the Mainland Ballet Theatre.

VICTOR WOLF

7769-J Frederic St.	Height-6'
Tampa, FL 87769	Weight-158 lbs.
813-555-3498	Age-22
	Citizenship- USA

Objective:
Acceptance into Canada's Royal Winnipeg Ballet's Professional Division School.

Highlights of experience:

- Fifty-two professional performances of *West Side Story* with Der Pfaltz Theatre in Germany.

- Featured as the Wolf in *Sleeping Beauty* (Johnson) for The Tampa Ballet.

- Danced in eight different productions with The University of South Florida's Dance Ensemble.

Education:

Victor's introduction to dance began at Der Pfaltz Theatre in preparation for performing the original choreography in a professional production of *West Side Story*.

While studying engineering at the University of South Florida, Victor was recruited into the dance department by former New York Ballet Theater's Mistress, Ingrid Walters. He was utilized extensively by the ballet department in eight different productions with the USF Dance Ensemble. His intensive studies over the past three years included: daily ballet technique from Ms. Walters, daily Limon technique from Liza Witner, *pas de deux*, men's variation, jazz, character, composition, music for dance, and dance history.

Victor has a natural ability for classical ballet and an enthusiastic work habit. With the potential to grow into a high-quality professional dancer, Victor promises to be a significant addition to any fine dance school.

Bad Examples

Amanda Wilson decided to audition for a ballet company and had her mother type the résumé. She could not help being biased when writing her daughter's résumé. Although Amanda's mother is an English teacher at the 54th Street High School, and an excellent typist, she did not know how to write an effective marketing piece.

Amanda's more impressive experience is her performances with San Francisco Ballet. Unfortunately, her mom buried this information deep within the résumé. Therefore, when John Medford, the artistic director of Ballet Georgia, glanced briefly at Amanda's résumé before an audition, he completely missed this important experience. He became under the impression that Amanda was a ballet student with no experience for a major ballet company.

Her second mistake was putting the color of her beautiful daughter's hair and eyes on the résumé. This information is unneeded on a dancer's résumé.

The names of the ballets need not be in quotation marks. Furthermore, Tomorrow and Brother Lament do not need the heading "Ballet" for the same reason the other ballets didn't need this heading—it's redundant.

Do not start your résumé with:

Ballet-10 years

Jazz- 4 years

Modern- 6 years

This is the sure sign of a rank amateur. Avoid it at all costs.

The title WITH WHOM AND CHOREOGRAPHER is confusing, and the layout of the résumé appears random and lacks forethought.

She also misspelled Coppelia and called the Nutcracker "The Nutcracker Sweet." Mistakes like these are unnecessary and unacceptable.

Fortunately, after missing the job at Ballet Georgia, Amanda reevaluated her résumé and had it rewritten. She now dances in Texas.

BAD EXAMPLE!

AMANDA WILSON
423 W. 55th St.
New York, NY 10023
212-555-7984

Birth date: 2-1-72
Height: 5'5"
Weight: 97#
Hair: Blonde
Eyes: Blue

TRAINING

Ballet- 8 years	Jazz- 10 years	Pas de deux- 3 years
Point- 8 years	Tap- 3 years	Dance history- 1 year
Character- 3 years	Modern- 3 years	Piano- 4 years

Mero Dance Academy
Frederick Johnson Dance Center

SUMMER SCHOOLS ATTENDED

1985, 1986	Pennsylvania School of Ballet
1987	San Francisco Ballet School
1988	School of American Ballet
1988	Northwest Ballet School
1989-1990	San Francisco Ballet School

Currently enrolled at San Francisco Ballet School.

TELEVISION

1986	Excerpts form "Coppelia" on PBS
1988	Excerpts form "Metro Dancin'" on PBS
1988	Commercial for "Metro Dancin'" on PBS
1988	Commercial for "Nutcracker" on PBS

PERFORMANCE EXPERIENCE

		WITH WHOM AND CHOREOGRAPHER
"Nutcracker Sweet"	1981 thru 1988 1989-1990	Mainland Ballet Theatre San Francisco Ballet Lew Christensen
"Copapelia"	1984,1985,1987	Mainland Ballet Theatre
"Sleeping Beauty"	1990	San Francisco Ballet Helgi Tomasson
"Divertimento"	1990	San Francisco Ballet Helgi Tomasson
"Metro Dancin'" Ballet "Tomorrow" Ballet "Brother Lament" Tap & Jazz "Jumpin' Nostalgia"	1988-1989	Mainland Ballet Theatre Edmund La Frick Kenny Red Zin Tansma

MUNICIPAL LIGHT OPERA

"East Side Story"	1986	Carl Jablonsky
"41nd Street"	1987	Jon Engstrom
"Bittter Charity"	1989	Hanna Jason

BAD EXAMPLE!

TOMMY DI MARIO
D.O.B: 3/14/68
HEIGHT: 5' 11"
WEIGHT: 158 LBS.

587 LUCASY DR.
ATLANTA GA, 30307
(404) 233-1388

PERFORMANCE EXPERIENCE:

BALLET	CHOREOGRAPHER	ROLE	LOCATION
ALLEGRO BRILLANTE	BALANCHINE	SOLOIST	BALLET FEZ
BILLY THE KID	LORING	CORPS	BALLET FEZ
CARMINA BURANA	FAULT	SOLOIST	WELLIND DANCE CO.
CASSANOVA	MINSKI	CORPS(FRIEND)	WELLIND DANCE CO.
COPPELIA	LUCER	SOLOIST	BALLET FEZ
ESCAPE	HOUDSTILL	CORPS	JAZZ FESTIVAL
GISELLE	LEE	SOLOIST	BALLET FEZ
KINETHSIS RED	OLD	PRINCIPAL	WELLIND DANCE CO.
LA FILLE MAL GARDE	BIRTHISTLE	CORPS	JAZZ FESTIVAL
LA SYLPHIDE	SOUTER	SOLOIST	BALLET FEZ
NUTCRACKER	WINSINGOR	SOLOIST	BALLET FEZ
" "	RODDEN	CORPS	JAZZ FESTIVAL
" "	SKULLARD	SOLOIST	WELLIND DANCE CO.
PAS DE DIX	WALTER	PRINCIPAL	BALLET FEZ
ROMEO AND JULIET	GRANT	PRINCIPAL	BALLET FEZ
REFLECTIONS	MELLON	SOLOIST	JAZZ FESTIVAL
SERENADE	BALANCHINE	CORPS	WELLIND DANCE CO.
SHAKESPEARE SUITE	ROCHERSETTI	SOLOIST	WELLIND DANCE CO.
SQUARE DANCE	BALANCHINE	CORPS	WELLIND DANCE CO.
TRIO ROUGE	ENAISESR	PRINCIPAL	WELLIND DANCE CO.

TRAINING:
1980-1985 SCHOOL OF HALIFAX DANCE ACADEMY
1984-1985 BALLET CONSERVITORY OF MARY JOHNSON
1988   JONNY SCHLEPPENHEIMER'S SCHOOL OF DANCE AND MIME

TEACHERS:
BALLET: JOHN LUCAS, ANNETTE RICHINGTON, DENISE ALEXANDER, MIKE ROBERTSON, MICHEL DAVIS, OTIS TOMPSON, UGGIE JOHNSON, EPPENHEIMER SCHLEP, ERIC WOLFRAM, BLANCA COMA, EARL STAFFORD, JOHN MEAN, MARDINE WASHINGTON, JORDEN MORTON, GALINA STOPHERINSKI, THOMAS RUSS, RAM TORISO, IORKA KAMURAINA
MODERN: GARY PAUL, MILES PEPPER, DONALD SCHROEDER, ICHIRIO TANAKA, LUKE G. SETTE
JAZZ: KEN CHILDERHOSE

About the Author

Eric Wolfram enjoyed the glamour of an international ballet career while performing with the critically acclaimed Royal Winnipeg Ballet and San Francisco Ballet. He appeared on renowned stages like the Paris Opera in Paris, The Kirov in St. Petersburg, Lincoln Center in New York, The Kennedy Center in Washington DC; as well as a hundred and fifty other theaters across the Americas and European continents. His articles appear in Dance Magazine and on Voiceofdance.com. He films dance in New York. He created two documentary films for San Francisco Ballet, which focus on the impact that San Francisco Ballet's Center for Dance Education had on some 3rd grade classrooms in San Francisco.

Your Dance Résumé

Order more copies

of this book?

Information about ordering more copies
of this book can be found at:

http://wolfram.org/writing/ydr/order.html